Classroom Assessment

Enhancing the Quality of Teacher Decision Making

Lorin W. Anderson
University of South Carolina

2003

LAWRENCE ERLBAUM ASSOCIATES, PUBLISHERS
Mahwah, New Jersey   London

Director, Editorial:	Lane Akers
Executive Assistant:	Bonita D'Amil
Cover Design:	Kathryn Houghtaling Lacey
Textbook Production Manager:	Paul Smolenski
Compositor:	LEA Book Production
Text and Cover Printer:	Hamilton Printing Company

This book was typeset in 10/12 pt. Palatino, Italic, Bold, and Bold Italic. The heads were typeset in Palatino.

Lawrence Erlbaum Associates, Inc., Publishers
10 Industrial Avenue
Mahwah, New Jersey 07430

Library of Congress Cataloging-in-Publication Data

Anderson, Lorin W.
Classroom assessment : enhancing the quality of teacher decision making / Lorin W. Anderson.

  p. cm.

Includes bibliographical references and index.
ISBN 0-8058-3602-0 (pbk. : alk. paper)
Educational tests and measurements. 2. Teaching—Decision making.
  I. Title.
LB3051 .A699   2002
371.26'4—dc21   2002074881
                                                     CIP

Books published by Lawrence Erlbaum Associates are printed on acid-free paper, and their bindings are chosen for strength and durability.

Printed in the United States of America
10 9 8 7 6 5 4 3 2

Classroom Assessment

Enhancing the Quality
of Teacher Decision Making

To Jo Anne

Contents

Preface

Assessment is the process of gathering information to make informed decisions. Before anyone engages in assessment, he or she must know why the assessment is being made (the purpose), what information is needed to make the decision (the basis), when the information is needed (the timing), and how the information is best collected (the method). The purpose of this book is to help practicing and prospective teachers gather better information and make better decisions. Consequently, unlike more conventional classroom assessment books, this book attempts to balance material about assessment with material about decision making. Although both assessment and decision making are important in their own right, this is a book about the link or connection between them.

This book also differs from more conventional classroom assessment books in the way it is organized. Actually, there are two differences in this regard. First, the organization is more sequential than many classroom assessment books. After an introductory chapter, the flow of the chapters moves from preparing (or selecting) assessment instruments to interpreting the results of those instruments to making decisions based on those results to communicating the results of the assessments and decisions. Second, the chapters are organized around substance, not method. That is, you do not see individual chapters on paper-and-pencil tests, performance assessments, observational methods, and the like. Rather, you see chapters on assessing achievement, classroom behavior, and effort. The relevant and appropriate methods are nested within these chapters.

In 1990, a joint committee of the American Federation of Teachers, National Council on Measurement in Education, and National Educational Association published a set of seven standards pertaining to what teachers should know about classroom assessment. I have considered each of these standards in writing this book. The standards and related chapter(s) are as follows:

1. Teachers should be skilled in choosing assessment methods appropriate for instructional decisions (Chapters 2, 3, 4, and 5).

2. Teachers should be skilled in developing assessment methods appropriate for instructional decisions (Chapters 2, 3, 4, and 5).
3. Teachers should be skilled in administering, scoring, and interpreting the results of both externally-produced and teacher produced assessment methods (Chapters 1, 4, and 6).
4. Teachers should be skilled in using assessment results when making decisions about individual students, planning teaching, developing curriculum, and school improvements (Chapters 1 and 7).
5. Teachers should be skilled in developing valid pupil grading procedures that use pupil assessments (Chapter 7).
6. Teachers should be skilled in communicating assessment results to students, parents, other lay audiences, and other educators (Chapter 8).
7. Teachers should be skilled in recognizing unethical, illegal, and otherwise inappropriate assessment methods and uses of assessment information (Chapter 1).

Throughout my 30-year career, I have had the privilege of knowing and, in some cases, working with some absolutely wonderful and brilliant people. In both thought and action, they have influenced me more than they know. In the fields of classroom assessment and classroom research, my thinking has been influenced greatly by Peter Airasian, Dave Berliner, Ben Bloom, Jere Brophy, Mick Dunkin, N. L. Gage, Phil Jackson, David Krathwohl, Jim Popham, Barak Rosenshine, Rick Stiggins, and Sam Stringfield. Thank you all!

Finally, I want to express my tremendous appreciation to Lane Akers, my editor at Lawrence Erlbaum Associates. I have had the pleasure of knowing Lane for about 15 years. He is truly one of the nicest people I have ever met. He is not a bad editor, either. Thanks, Lane.

—*Lorin W. Anderson*

Classroom Assessment

Enhancing the Quality
of Teacher Decision Making

CHAPTER ONE

Introduction to Classroom Assessment

"What makes a good teacher?" This question has been debated at least since formal schooling began, if not long before. It is a difficult question to answer because, as Rabinowitz and Travers (1953) pointed out almost a half-century ago, the good teacher "does not exist pure and serene, available for scientific scrutiny, but is instead a fiction of the minds of men" (p. 586). Some have argued that good teachers possess certain traits, qualities, or characteristics. These teachers are understanding, friendly, responsible, enthusiastic, imaginative, and emotionally stable (Ryans, 1960). Others have suggested that good teachers interact with their students in certain ways and use particular teaching practices. They give clear directions, ask higher order questions, give feedback to students, and circulate among students as they work at their desks, stopping to provide assistance as needed (Brophy & Good, 1986). Still others have argued that good teachers facilitate learning on the part of their students. Not only do their students learn, but they also are able to demonstrate their learning on standardized tests (Medley, 1982). What each of us means when we use the phrase *good teacher*, then, depends primarily on what we value in or about teachers.

Since the 1970s, there has been a group of educators and researchers who have argued that the key to being a good teacher lies in the decisions that teachers make:

> Any teaching act is the result of a decision, whether conscious or unconscious, that the teacher makes after the complex cognitive processing of available information. This reasoning leads to the hypothesis that *the* basic teaching skill is decision making. (Shavelson, 1973, p. 18); (*emphasis* added)

In addition to emphasizing the importance of decision making, Shavelson made a critically important point. Namely, teachers make their decisions "after the complex cognitive processing of available information." Thus, there is an essential link between available information and decision making. Using the terminology of educational researchers, information is a **necessary, but not sufficient** condition for good decision making. In other words, without information, good decisions are difficult. Yet simply having the information does not mean that good decisions are made. As Bussis, Chittenden, and Amarel (1976) noted:

> Decision-making is invariably a subjective, human activity involving value judgments ... placed on whatever evidence is available.... Even when there is virtual consensus of the "facts of the matter," such facts do not automatically lead to decisions regarding future action. People render decisions; information does not. (p. 19)

As we see throughout this book, teachers have many sources of information they can use in making decisions. Some are better than others, but all are typically considered at some point in time. The critical issue facing teachers, then, is what information to use and how to use it to make the best decisions possible in the time available. Time is important because many decisions need to be made before we have all the information we would like to have.

UNDERSTANDING TEACHERS' DECISIONS

The awareness that a decision needs to be made is often stated in the form of a *should* question (e.g., "What should I do in this situation?"). Here are some examples of the everyday decisions facing teachers:

1. Should I send a note to Barbara's parents informing them that she constantly interrupts the class and inviting them to a conference to discuss the problem?
2. Should I stop this lesson to deal with the increasing noise level in the room or should I just ignore it, hoping it will go away?
3. What should I do to get LaKeisha back on task?
4. Should I tell students they will have a choice of activities tomorrow if they complete their group projects by the end of the class period?
5. What grade should I give Jorge on his essay?
6. Should I move on to the next unit or should I spend a few more days reteaching the material before moving on?

Although all of these are *should* questions, they differ in three important ways. First, the odd-numbered questions deal with individual students, whereas the even-numbered questions deal with the entire class. Second, the first two questions deal with classroom behavior, the second two questions with student effort, and the third two questions with student achievement. Third, some of the decisions (e.g., Questions 2, 3, and, perhaps, 6) must be made on the spot, whereas for others (e.g., Questions 1, 4, and, to a certain extent, 5) teachers have more time to make their decisions. These *should* questions (and their related decisions), then, can be differentiated in terms of (a) the *focus* of the decision (individual student or group), (b) the *basis* for the decision (classroom behavior, effort, or achievement), and (c) the *timing* of the decision (immediate or longer term). This structure of teacher decision making is shown in Fig. 1.1.

Virtually every decision that teachers make concerning their students can be placed in one of the cells of Fig. 1.1. For example, the first question concerns the classroom behavior of an individual student, which the teacher can take some time to make. This question, then, would be placed in the cell corresponding with classroom behavior (the basis for the decision) of an individual student (the focus of the decision), with a reasonable amount of time to make the decision (the timing of the decision). In contrast, the sixth question concerns the achievement of a class of students and requires the teacher to make a rather immediate decision. This question, then, would be placed in the cell corresponding with achievement (the basis for the decision) of a class of students (the focus of the decision), with some urgency attached to the making of the decision (the timing of the decision).

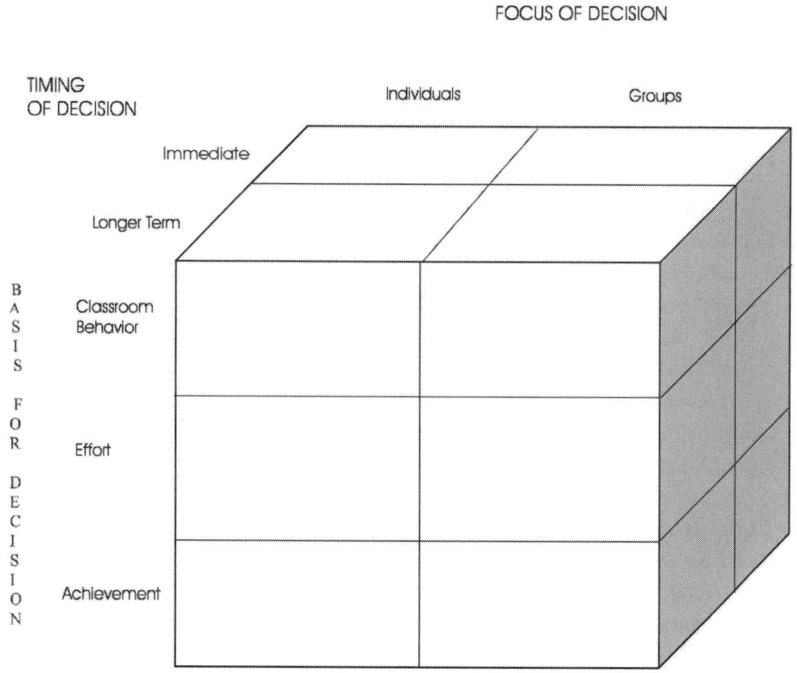

FIG. 1.1 Structure of teacher decision making.

UNDERSTANDING HOW TEACHERS MAKE DECISIONS

On what basis do teachers make decisions? They have several possibilities. First, they can decide to do what they have always done:

- "How should I teach these students? I should teach them the way I've always taught them. I put a couple of problems on the overhead projector and work them for the students. Then I give them a worksheet containing similar problems and tell them to complete the worksheet and to raise their hands if they have any trouble."
- "What grade should I assign Billy? Well, if his cumulative point total exceeds 92, he gets an 'A.' If not, he gets a lower grade in accordance with his cumulative point total. I tell students about my grading scale at the beginning of the year."

Teachers who choose to stay with the status quo tend to do so because they believe what they are doing is the right thing to do, they have become comfortable doing it, or they cannot think of anything else to do. Decisions that require us to change often cause a great deal of discomfort, at least initially.

Second, teachers can make decisions based on real and practical constraints, such as time, materials and equipment, state mandates, and personal frustration:

- "How much time should I spend on this unit? Well, if I'm going to complete the course syllabus, I will need to get to *Macbeth* by February at the latest. That means I can't spend more than three weeks on this unit."
- "How should I teach my students? I would love to incorporate computer technology. But I only have two computers in my classroom. What can I do with two computers and 25 students? So I think I'll just stay with the 'tried and true' until we get more computers."
- "What can I do to motivate Horatio? I could do a lot more if it weren't for those state standards. I have to teach this stuff because the state says I have to, whether he is interested in learning it or not."
- "Where does Hortense belong? Anywhere but in my class. I've tried everything I know … talked with the parents … talked with the guidance counselor. I just need to get her out of my class."

Although maintaining the status quo and operating within existing constraints are both viable decision-making alternatives, this is a book about making decisions based on information about students. At its core, ***assessment*** means gathering information about students that can be used to aid teachers in the decision-making process.

SOURCES OF INFORMATION

It seems almost trivial to point out that different decisions require different information. Nonetheless, this point is often forgotten or overlooked by far too many teachers and administrators. How do teachers get the information about students that they need to make decisions? In general, they have three alternatives. First, they can examine information that already exists, such as information included in students' permanent files. These files typically include students' grades, standardized test scores, health reports, and the like. Second, teachers can observe students in their *natural habitats*—as students sit in their classrooms, interact with other students, read on their own, complete written work at their desks or tables, and so on. Finally, they can assign specific tasks to students (e.g., ask them questions, tell them to make or do something) and see how well they perform these tasks. Let us consider each of these alternatives.

Existing Information

After the first year or two of school, a great deal of information is contained in a student's permanent file. Examples include:

- health information (e.g., immunizations, handicapping conditions, chronic diseases);
- transcripts of courses taken and grades earned in those courses;
- written comments made by teachers;
- standardized test scores;
- disciplinary referrals;
- correspondence between home and school;
- participation in extracurricular activities;
- portions of divorce decrees pertaining to child custody and visitation rights; and
- arrest records.

This information can be used to make a variety of decisions. Information that a child is a diabetic, for example, can help a teacher make the proper decision should the child begin to exhibit unusual behavior. Information about child custody enables an administrator to make the right decision when a noncustodial parent comes to school to pick up the child. Information about a child's grades can be used to determine whether the child should be placed on the Principal's List or Honor Roll. Information about previous disciplinary referrals typically provides the basis for determining the proper punishment following an incident of misbehavior. Information obtained from standardized test scores is used in many schools to decide whether a child should be placed in a class for gifted and talented students or whether the child is in need of academic assistance.

Although all of these examples pertain to individual students, it is possible and, in many cases, desirable to combine (or aggregate) the data to provide information about groups of students. How many students are on the Principal's List or Honor Roll? Are there the same numbers of boys and girls? Have these numbers (or percentages) changed over the past several years? How many disciplinary referrals have occurred this year? Are the numbers of referrals the same for Whites, Blacks, Hispanics, Asians, and so on? Are the numbers of referrals increasing, decreasing, or staying the same? How many students score in the highest quarter nationally on the standardized tests … in the lowest quarter … above the national average? Are the scores the same for Whites, Blacks, Hispanics, Asians, and so on? For boys and girls? On average, are the scores increasing, decreasing, or remaining the same?

Interestingly, some administrators and teachers are concerned about the use of the information contained in students' permanent records to make decisions. Specifically, they are concerned that this information may bias the person accessing it. Because of this bias, for example, a student may be improperly labeled as a *troublemaker* and treated accordingly. Alternatively, a teacher may bring a bias to the information contained in a student's permanent file. Such a teacher may search through the file for information supporting his or her perception that the student is incapable of learning the material being covered in class. As we shall see throughout this book, the problems of the misinterpretation and misuse of information are serious indeed. However, these problems are no more likely to occur with information contained in students' permanent files than with any other information source.

Naturalistic Observations

There is ample evidence that many of the immediate decisions that teachers make are based on their observations of students in their classrooms (Clark & Peterson, 1986). In fact, the available evidence suggests that teachers make some type of decision every 2 minutes they are in their classrooms and rely heavily on this observational information to do so (Fogarty, Wang, & Creek, 1982; Jackson, 1968). The logic of this decision-making process is as follows:

1. If my students are not disruptive, they are complying with the classroom rules.
2. If my students are paying attention, they are probably learning.
3. So, if my students are not disruptive and are paying attention, then I shall continue to teach the way I am teaching since my instruction is probably effective.

However, if students are engaged in disruptive behavior **or** are not pay-ing attention, then there is a need to do something different. Yet to do something different requires that a decision about what to do differently be made and carried out. If, for example, a fair number of students have puzzled looks on their faces, the teacher may decide to go back over the material one more time. If only 3 of the 25 students in the class have com-pleted a written assignment, the teacher may decide to give them 10 more minutes to complete it. If Dennis seems to be daydreaming, the teacher may decide to call on Dennis to answer a question. Finally, if Denise is sit-ting at her desk with her hand raised, the teacher may decide to walk to her desk and give her some help.

When making decisions about groups of students, not every student need be included in the decision-making process. For example, the afore-mentioned puzzled looks may be on the faces of only five or six students. About 30 years ago, Dahloff (1971) suggested that teachers used *steering groups* to help them make decisions about the pace of instruction. These groups, typically composed of four or five students, literally steer the pac-ing through the curriculum units. If it appears that this group of students got it, the teacher moves on. If not, he or she reviews the material one more time or tries a different approach to get the material across. Quite obvi-ously, the pace of instruction is directly related to the academic composi-tion of the steering group. Including higher achieving students in the steering group results in more rapid pacing; the reverse is true for groups composed primarily of lower achieving students.

Naturalistic observations are an important and quite reasonable way for teachers to get the information they need to make decisions because teach-ers are constantly engaged in observation. In addition, the feedback they re-ceive from observations is immediate, unlike test data that may require days, weeks, or months (in the case of statewide achievement tests or commercial norm-referenced tests) to process. However, information obtained via natu-ralistic observation can be misleading. The puzzled looks may be a ploy on the part of students to stop the teacher from moving forward. The reason that only 3 of the 25 students have completed the assignment may be that the rest of the students do not know how to do the work. In this case, giving them 10 additional minutes without some instructional intervention would be a waste of time. Dennis may be concentrating, not daydreaming. Denise may be stretching, not raising her hand for assistance.

Assessment Tasks

Following tradition, if teachers want to know whether their students have learned what they were supposed to learn, how students feel about what they are learning, how they perceive their classroom environment, and so on, they administer quizzes, tests, or questionnaires. These assessment instruments typically contain a series of items (e.g., questions to be answered, incomplete sentences to be completed, matches to be made between entries in one column and those in another). In some cases, the instrument may contain a single item. In these cases, this item often requires that the student produce an extended response (e.g., write an essay about ...; demonstrate that ...). To simplify matters, we refer to all of the items included on these instruments, regardless of their structure, format, or number, as *assessment tasks*. Occasionally, when needed to maintain the flow of the writing, "item" also will be used.

Different tasks may require different responses from students. The nature of the required response is inherent in the verb included in the task description ("**Write** an essay about ...") or in the directions given to students about the tasks ("**Circle** the option that ..."). In general, these verbs ask students to perform some action (e.g., write, demonstrate) or select from among possible responses to the task (e.g., circle, choose). Not surprisingly, the first set of tasks is referred to as *performance tasks*, whereas the second set of tasks is referred to as *selection tasks*.

Which tasks we should use to get the information we need to make a decision depends primarily on the type of information we need to make the decision. For example, if we need information about how well students have memorized the authors of a series of novels, it seems reasonable to use a selection task—specifically, one presented to students in a matching format (with titles of novels listed in one column and novelists listed in another). However, if we need information about how well students can explain a current event (e.g., nationwide increases or decreases in school violence) in terms of various historical and contemporary factors, a performance task (e.g., a research report) may be more appropriate. Finally, suppose we want information about how well students like school. In this case, either selection tasks (such as those included on traditional attitude scales) or performance tasks (such as a written response to the prompt "Write a brief essay describing the things you like most and least about this school") could be used. This last example illustrates that assessment tasks are not limited to what traditionally has been termed the *cognitive domain*. This is an important point, one that reappears throughout this book.

However, contrary to what you might read elsewhere, certain forms of assessment tasks are no better or worse than others. There are people who relentlessly *bash* multiple-choice tests. There are those who advocate performance assessment with what can only be termed *religious zeal*. Of course, there are those who believe that any form of standardized testing is bad. Based on my 30 years of experience, I have learned an important lesson (one that you hopefully will learn in much less time). Assessment tasks are like tools in a carpenter's toolbox. Like a good carpenter, a good assessor has a variety of tools that he or she learns to use well to accomplish the intended purpose(s). Just as a carpenter may strive to build the best house possible, a teacher should strive to make the best decisions possible. One important element of good decision making is the quality of information on which the decision is based.

Before we move to a discussion of the quality of information obtained via assessment, however, one final comment about assessment tasks is in order. Many assessment tasks look much like what may be termed *learning tasks*. Consider the following task.

> You find the following artifacts during an archeological dig. [Pictures of six artifacts are shown here]. Determine the likely purpose and origin of each artifact. Considering all six artifacts, describe the likely traits of the people who made or used them. (Adapted from www.relearning.org.)

This certainly is a task. Specifically, the students are to examine the six artifacts and, based on this examination, (a) determine their likely purpose and origin, and (b) describe the likely traits of the people who made or used them. Yet, is this an assessment task? Unfortunately, you cannot answer this question by looking at it no matter how closely, carefully, or often. To answer this question, you have to know or infer why the task was given to the students in the first place. If the task were given to help students learn how to determine the purposes and origins of artifacts, and how to determine the likely traits of the people who made or used them, then it is a *learning task* (because it is intended to help students learn). In contrast, if it is given to see how well students have learned how to determine the purposes and origins of artifacts, and the likely traits of the people who made or used them after some period of instruction, then it would be an *assessment task*.

The confusion between learning tasks and assessment tasks looms large in many classrooms because tasks are such an integral part of classroom instruction. If you enter almost any classroom, you are likely to see students completing worksheets, solving problems contained in textbooks, constructing models of theaters or atoms, or engaging in experiments. Because they are assigned to students, these tasks are often called *assignments* (which is shorthand for *assigned tasks*).

On the surface, the issue here is quite simple. Whatever they are called, are they given to promote or facilitate learning or are they given to assess how well learning has occurred? In reality, however, the issue is quite complex. Teachers often assess student learning while students are engaged in learning tasks. In this situation, the task serves both learning (for the students) and assessment (for the teacher) purposes.

Consider the archeological dig example previously mentioned. Suppose for a moment that it truly is a learning task. That is, the task is intended to help students learn how to examine historical artifacts in terms of their purposes and origins, as well as the traits of the people who made or used them. Suppose further that students are to work on this task in pairs. As they work, the teacher circulates among the students visually monitoring their progress or lack thereof. As problems are noted via this observational assessment, the teacher stops and offers suggestions, hints, or clues. At the end of the class period, the teacher collects the assignment, reads through what the students have written, writes comments, and offers suggestions for improvement. At the start of the next class period, the teacher gives the assignment back to the students and tells them to revise their work based on the feedback he or she has provided them.

Some would argue this is the perfect blend of instruction and assessment because the task serves both purposes: learning and assessment. Others have argued that the link between instruction and assessment is so tight in this situation that there is no independent assessment of whether the intended learning actually occurred (Anderson et al., 2001). Because teachers often provide assistance to students as they work on learning tasks, the quality of students' performance on learning tasks is influenced by the students as well as their teachers. In other words, when assessments are made based on student performance on learning tasks (rather than specifically designated assessment tasks), teachers are simultaneously assessing the quality of student learning and their own teaching.

THE QUALITY OF INFORMATION

Before there were classroom assessment books, there were tests and measurement books. If you were to read these tests and measurement books, you would find chapters, sections of chapters, or, occasionally, multiple chapters written about validity, reliability, and objectivity. Unfortunately, the chapter titles in these books are sometimes misleading. For example, you may find a chapter entitled "Test Validity." The title suggests that validity is inherent in the tests themselves. This simply is not true. Validity pertains to the *test scores*. Stated somewhat differently, validity is an indicator of the quality of the information obtained by administering a test to a student or group of students.

All three concepts – validity, reliability, and objectivity – have to do with the quality of the information obtained from tests or other assessment instruments or methods. Because these concepts have long historical standing in the field, we review each of them briefly. The focus of this brief review is on their practical application to classroom assessment. To aid in the discussion, we rely on two examples: one concerning individual student achievement and the other concerning individual student effort.

Validity

In general terms, *validity* is the extent to which the information obtained from an assessment instrument (e.g., test) or method (e.g., observation) enables you to accomplish the purpose for which the information was collected. In terms of classroom assessment, the purpose is to inform a decision. For example, a teacher wants to decide on the grade to be assigned to a student or a teacher wants to know what he or she should do to get a student to work harder.

To simplify the grading example, let us assume that we are assigning a grade based on a student's performance on a single test. Let us further assume that the test represents a unit of material that requires about 3 weeks to complete. Finally, let us assume that we want the grade to reflect how well the student has achieved the stated unit objectives. What are the validity issues in this example? First, we want to make sure that the items on the test (i.e., the assessment tasks) are directly related to the unit objectives. This is frequently termed *content validity*. Second, we want to make sure that the proportions of the items related to the various objectives correspond with the emphasis given to those objectives in the unit. This is frequently referred to as *instructional validity*. Third, we want to assign the grade based on how well the students have mastered the objectives, not based on how well they perform relative to other students. In common parlance, we want to make a *criterion-referenced*, not a *norm-referenced* decision. To do this, we need defensible performance standards. The greater the content validity, the greater the instructional validity and the more defensible the performance standards, the greater the overall validity of the information obtained from the test for the purpose of assigning a grade to a student.

Let us move to the effort example. By phrasing the question the way we did (i.e., What should I do to get this student to work harder?), we have already made one decision—namely, that the student in question does not work very hard (or certainly as hard as you, the teacher, would like). On what basis did we arrive as this determination? Typically, the information used to make this decision comes from naturalistic observations. "The student is easily distracted." "The student neither completes not turns in homework." The initial validity question in this case concerns the validity of the inference about lack of effort made based on the observational information.

Effort is what psychologists refer to as a construct. That is, it is a hypothetical or constructed idea that helps us make sense of what we see and hear. From an assessment point of view, constructs must be linked with indicators. *Distractibility* and *no homework* are negative indicators. That is, they are indicators of a lack of effort. The issue before us is whether they are valid indicators of a lack of effort. To address this issue, we must consider alternative hypotheses. Perhaps distractibility is a function of some type of neurological disorder. Similarly, no homework may be a function of a lack of the knowledge needed to complete the homework. These alternative hypotheses must be examined and subsequently ruled out if we are to accept that distractibility and no homework are valid indicators of a lack of effort. This is the process of construct validity.

Yet this is only part of the validity puzzle. The question raised by the teacher is what he or she should do to get the student to worker harder. To answer this question, we need additional information—information not available by means of observation. Specifically, we need to know *why* the student is not putting forth sufficient effort. We explore the *why* question in greater detail throughout the book.

Reliability

Reliability is the consistency of the information obtained from one or more assessments. Some writers equate reliability with dependability, which conjures up a common-sense meaning of the term. A reliable person is a dependable one—a person who can be counted on in a variety of situations and at various times. Similarly, reliable information is information that is consistent across tasks, settings, times, and/or assessors. Because the issue of consistency across assessors typically falls under the heading of *objectivity*, it is discussed a bit later.

Let us return to the grading example introduced in the validity section. Continuing with our assumptions, let us suppose that the test is a mathematics test and consists of a single item (If $.2x + 7.2 = 12$, what is the value of x?). Furthermore, suppose that the major objective of the unit was for students to learn to solve for unknowns in number sentences (content validity) and that all but 10% of time devoted to the unit focused on learning to solve for unknowns in number sentences (instructional validity). Finally, suppose the grading was pass or fail. That is, if the student arrives at the right answer (i.e., $x = 24$), he or she is assigned a grade of *pass* (regardless of how many other students got the item right). Otherwise, a grade of *fail* is assigned.

Items such as this one would have a high degree of validity for the purpose of assigning student a grade. Yet where does a single-item test stand in terms of reliability? How much confidence would you place in the results of a single-item test? Hopefully, not a great deal. The use of multiple items permits us to investigate consistency across tasks. Typically, the greater the number of tasks (obviously to some limit), the greater the reliability of the information we obtain from a student's performance on those tasks, which in turn is used to make inferences about that student's achievement on the unit objectives.

We may be interested in other types of consistency of student task performance. For example, we can readminister the test in 2 weeks to examine the consistency of the information over time. We may arrange for two administrative conditions, one in the regular classroom and the other in the library, to see whether the information remains consistent across settings. Finally, we can have two different tests, each composed of a random sample of all possible items that could be written for this objective (e.g., $.4x - 6 = -2$; $15x + 10 = 160$; $1.8x - 18 = 0$; $3x + 2 = 38$; $-6x - 6 = -60$; $24x + 24 = 480$). By administering the two tests, we could determine whether students' scores are the same on the two tests or whether a student's score depends on the particular test that was administered. All of these are ways to examine the reliability of the information we gather when we assess students.

Turning to the effort example, the initial determination that the student was lacking effort can be subjected to the same type of examination. We can observe the student in different classes (settings), learning different subjects (tasks), and in the morning and the afternoon (time). By comparing the different results, we may learn that the student is distractible and fails to turn in completed homework only when he or she is in my class. In other words, I may be a source of the problem. If so, this increased understanding moves me toward answering the primary question: What can I do to get this student to work harder?

Unreliability is a problem because it creates errors. More specifically, unreliability decreases the precision with which the measurement is made. Quite clearly, imprecise measurement is not a good thing. In classroom assessment, however, as the previous example shows, a lack of reliability (i.e., consistency) may be informative. Knowing what accounts for the inconsistency of the information that we collect may provide the understanding we need to begin to solve the problem and arrive at a defensible decision.

Most of the time, however, having reliable information is a good thing. When grades need to be assigned, having consistency of student performance across assignments and tests makes the decision to assign a grade of, say, "B" more defensible. How do we justify a grade of "B" on a report card if the student has received grades of "A" on all homework and three quizzes and a grade of "C" on the two projects? We can argue that it is best to compute an average when confronted with such inconsistency, but that does not deal with the inconsistency per se. The inconsistency can result from differential validity (i.e., the quizzes and projects are measuring different things) or a lack of reliability (assuming the same thing is being measured). Regardless of the cause of inconsistency, it must be dealt with in some way.

Reliability of assessment information is particularly important when potentially life-altering decisions are made about students. For example, a decision to classify a student as a special education student must be based on information that is remarkably consistent over tasks, time, settings, and observers/assessors.

The point here is that, like validity, the reliability of information must be examined in the context of the purpose for which the information is gathered. A single case of **documented** sexual harassment by one student of another is generally sufficient grounds for suspension, expulsion, and, perhaps, criminal prosecution. For other qualities and characteristics (e.g., laziness), however, information taken from several occasions and situations is needed.

Objectivity

In the field of tests and measurement, objectivity means that the scores assigned by different people to students' responses to items included on a quiz, test, homework assignment, and so on are identical or, at the very least, highly similar. If a student is given a multiple-choice test that has an accompanying answer key, then anyone using the answer key to score the tests should arrive at the same score. Hence, multiple-choice tests (along with true–false tests, matching tests, and most short answer tests) are referred to as *objective tests*. Once again, as in the case of test validity, this is a bit of a misnomer. It is the scores on the tests, not the tests per se, that are objective.

The importance of objectivity in assessment can perhaps best be understood if we consider the alternative. For example, suppose that a student's score on a particular test depends more on the person scoring the test than it does on the student's responses to the assessment tasks. Quite clearly, this is not an acceptable condition.

As might be expected, concerns for objectivity are particularly acute with performance tasks (e.g., essays, projects). However, there are several ways to increase the objectivity of scoring the responses made by students to these assessment tasks. The three major ways are to:

- use a common set of scoring or evaluation criteria;
- use a scoring rubric and so-called *anchors* to enhance the meaning of each criterion (see chap. 4); and
- provide sufficient training to those responsible for doing the scoring.

Within the larger assessment context, the concept of *objectivity* can, and probably should, be replaced by the concept of *corroboration* (see chap. 7). This is quite evident in the sexual harassment example mentioned earlier. Although it only takes one instance of sexual harassment to render a decision of school suspension or expulsion, we must be certain that the information we have concerning that instance is corroborated by others.

ISSUES IN THE ASSESSMENT OF STUDENTS

Because assessment is linked to decision making, and because an increasing number of decisions made about students have serious, long-term consequences, teachers must take assessment seriously. In this section, we consider three issues teachers should be aware of and must address in some fashion: (a) ethics of assessment, (b) preparing students for assessment, and (c) standardization and accommodation.

The Ethics of Assessment

Ethical matters pertain to all types of assessment by virtue of the fact that information about individual students is collected. In fact, because teaching is partly a moral enterprise, ethics pertain to virtually every aspect of classroom life. Both the National Education Association and the American Federation of Teachers have issued ethical standards for teachers' relations with their students. Four of these are particularly applicable to formal assessment.

First, strive to obtain information that is highly valid, reliable, and objective before making important decisions that affect students. For example, a semester grade should be based on a student's performance on assessment tasks that are clearly linked with important learning objectives. Similarly, referring a student for additional testing or for placement in a particular program requires that assessment information is obtained in multiple situations and on several occasions.

Second, recognize the limitations inherent in making decisions based on information obtained from assessments. Despite all efforts to secure the most valid, reliable, and objective information, errors occur and mistakes are made. Hence, multiple sources of information generally provide a more defensible basis for making important decisions about students. Corroboration, consistency, and concern for consequences are three Cs that are extremely useful in good decision making (see chap. 7).

Third, do not use information obtained from assessments to demean or ridicule students. Although this should go without saying, it is important to keep in mind. In an attempt to motivate a student to do better in the future, a teacher may make statements that can be construed as demeaning by the students (e.g., "Do you enjoy always getting the lowest score in the class?"). Also out of frustration, teachers may make comments they later regret. Following a classroom observation, I remember asking one teacher if she was unaware that one student slept through the entire lesson. Her response, overheard by several students, was, "It's better to let sleeping dogs lie."

Fourth, do not disclose assessment information about students unless disclosure serves a compelling professional purpose or is required by law.

Students have the right of privacy. The Family Educational Rights to Privacy Act (FERPA), enacted in 1974, was intended to protect students and their parents from having their personal and academic records made public without their consent. FERPA requires that:

- Student records must be kept confidential among the teacher, student, and student's parents or guardian.
- Written consent must be obtained from the student's parents before disclosing that student's records to a third party.
- Parents must be allowed to challenge the accuracy of the information kept in their children's records.
- Students who have reached the age of 18 must be accorded the same rights formerly granted to their parents.

It is important to note that the term *records* as used in the legislation includes such things as hand-written notes, grade books, computer printouts, taped interviews, and performances (Gallagher, 1998).

Preparing Students for Assessment

To obtain the best information possible, students should be prepared for each formal assessment—that is, an assessment consisting of a set of assessment tasks. A set of guidelines that can help teachers prepare students for formal assessments is shown in Table 1.1.

The first guideline is that students should be made aware of the assessment. They should know when it will take place as well as its purpose, structure, format, and content. Students should be given sufficient information to answer the basic journalistic questions: who, where, where, why, when, and how.

The second guideline concerns the emotional tone established for the assessment—a tone quite often set by teachers. Students should be told to do their best (on assessments of achievements) or reminded of the importance of indicating their true beliefs and feelings (e.g., on affective assessments related to effort). In addition, they should be reminded of the importance of the assessment in their own lives. Does one half of their grade depend on their performance? Are their chances of entering the college of their choice affected by their performance?

The third through fifth guidelines are concerned with the way in which students approach the assessment once it begins. They should read and follow the directions. They should pace themselves, periodically checking their progress relative to the available time. They should skip over those items they do not know or understand, returning to them if they have sufficient time.

TABLE 1.1
Guidelines for Preparing Students for Formal Assessments

1. Announce the assessment in advance and inform students of the purpose, structure, format, and content of the assessment instrument or procedure.

2. Approach the assessment positively, yet honestly.

3. Remind students to pay careful attention to the directions and follow the directions exactly.

4. Tell students to pace themselves so they complete the entire assessment.

5. Tell students to skip over items if they do not know the answer and come back to them later, time permitting. If they do get back to those items, tell them to make educated guesses for as many items as possible in the time remaining. (By an educated guess, I mean that students are certain that one or more of the choices of answers is definitely wrong.)

6. For essay tests, tell students to plan and organize their essays before writing them.

7. Tell students to be in good physical and mental condition for the assessment (e.g., to get a good night's sleep, to eat a good breakfast). If it is high-stakes assessment, send a note home reminding parents/guardians about the upcoming assessment.

The sixth guideline concerns essay examinations, while the seventh concerns high-stakes tests. Students should prepare an outline of their major points prior to writing the essay. If the assessment is high stakes (i.e., the results of the assessment are likely to have serious consequences for the students), sufficient rest and nutrition should be encouraged, even to the point of reminding parents of this.

Some readers might suggest that these guidelines are more important for secondary school students than for elementary school students. Although this may have been the case in the past, it is no longer true. Critical decisions are made about students based on assessment information obtained as early as first grade. Is this student ready for school? The assessment needed to make this decision typically focuses on achievement and effort. Does this student have attention deficit-hyperactivity disorder (ADHD)? The assessment needed to make this decision focuses primarily on classroom behavior and, to a lesser extent, effort. Should this student be placed in a special education program? Depending on the program being considered, this assessment may focus on achievement, effort, or classroom behavior. An increasing number of decisions that affect a child's future, both in and out of school, are made in the early grades. We need to prepare students for these decisions, and we need to get them (the decisions) right.

Standardization and Accommodation

There seems to be a great deal of confusion about the term *standardization*. Some educators would lead you to believe that the term applies only to high-stakes tests. Others would have you believe that it applies only to so-called *norm-referenced tests*. Still others would have you believe that only commercial testing companies have standardized tests. In point of fact, the term *standardized* applies to virtually all formal assessments.

Standardization simply means that the **same** set of assessment tasks is given to all students in the **same** order under the **same** assessment conditions. This definition is consistent with the dictionary definition of *standardized*—that is, uniform. Using this definition, most teacher-made tests and quizzes are standardized, as are most structured observation forms and student self-report instruments.

There are at least two practical reasons for standardization. First, only one instrument needs to be prepared. This saves time at the front end of the assessment process. Second, standardization permits large-group administration of instruments. This saves time at the back end of the assessment process.

At the same time, however, there have been an increasing number of calls for nonstandardization. Most of these fall within the general category of accommodation. Let us be clear from the outset. Accommodation deals with the **how**, not the **what**, of assessment. This critical distinction between how and what has been upheld by two federal rulings (Anderson v. Banks, 1981; Brookhart v. Illinois Board of Education, 1982).

To better understand this distinction, let us look at the kinds of accommodations that are appropriate. A list of possible accommodations is shown in Table 1.2. These accommodations can be understood in one of two ways. First, we can examine them in terms of whether they focus on the administrative conditions, the way in which the tasks are presented to the students, or the way in which students respond to the tasks. Within this framework, Accommodations 1 to 3 address the administrative conditions, Accommodations 4 to 6 address the presentation of tasks, and Accommodations 7 and 8 address the responses to the tasks.

Second, and perhaps more important, the accommodations can be examined in terms of the problem they are trying to solve. When examined in this way, the following pattern emerges:

- Auditory difficulties (Accommodation 6);
- Visual difficulties (Accommodations 4, 5, 6, and 8);
- Time constraint difficulties (Accommodation 1);

TABLE 1.2
Possible Student Accommodations

1. Provide extra time for the assessment.
2. Change the setting of the assessment to cut down on distractions.
3. Make the assessment "open book," including notes.
4. Read directions orally and give students ample opportunity to ask questions.
5. Read questions to students.
6. Use a special edition of the assessment (e.g., large print, audiotapes).
7. Give examples of how to respond to the tasks.
8. Permit students to respond orally, audiotaping their responses.

- Behavioral/anxiety difficulties (Accommodations 2, 4, and 7); and
- Memory difficulties (Accommodation 3).

This way of examining the issue of accommodation returns us to one of the major points made earlier in this chapter. Solving problems requires that we move beyond description of the problem to an explanation of its causes. Using a large-print edition of the assessment or reading the directions and/or questions to students is only appropriate for students with visual or reading difficulties. It is unlikely to help those students whose problems stem from auditory, time constraint, behavioral/anxiety, or memory difficulties.

One final matter concerning nonstandardization must be addressed before moving to the next chapter. In addition to matching the hypothesized cause of the problem, the reasonableness of some accommodations depends on the nature of the assessment per se. If we are assessing reading comprehension, then reading the items to students leads to an invalid assessment. If accommodations are to be made, then the what of assessment needs to be changed: Reading comprehension would have to be replaced with "understanding text" (Gredler, 1999, p. 254). If we are assessing students' ability to recall mathematical or scientific formulas, then the accommodation of giving students the formulas to "lessen reliance on memory" (Airasian, 1997, p. 204) would be inappropriate. However, we are assessing students' ability to apply mathematical or scientific formulas, then this accommodation would be quite appropriate.

Unfortunately, the topic of accommodation is discussed primarily in the context of special education. As Phillips (1994) noted, however, allowing all students access to useful accommodations may be fair to low-achieving students as well. Although by law they are not entitled to supportive accommodations, they often would benefit by having this opportunity to demonstrate their capabilities within traditional, standardized assessment settings.

ASSESSMENT AND DECISION MAKING

As mentioned earlier in this chapter, high-quality information does not guarantee that the wisest of decisions are made. At the same time, however, wise decisions generally require high-quality information. So what is the relationship between assessment and decision making? Where does evaluation fit into this picture? Once again, the answers to these questions depend on the type of decision that needs to be made.

In addition to the difference among decisions shown in Fig. 1.1, decisions can also be differentiated in terms of what might be termed *straightforward decisions* and what might be termed *problematic decisions*. Straightforward decisions are those that can reasonably be made based on the information available at the time. Decisions pertaining to the grading of students tend to be straightforward decisions. Other rather straightforward decisions are how to arrange classrooms, where to focus time and effort, and whether to seek advice and counsel from others.

Problematic decisions, in contrast, are those that typically require information beyond the initial information available. Decisions as to how best to motivate students tend to be problematic decisions. We may make a fairly straightforward inference that a student is unmotivated based on observational data. The student does not come to class and, when in class, he or she sleeps. The student rarely hands in assignments and the assignments turned in are of poor quality. In common parlance, we have *identified the problem*. However, what we do to solve the problem is not at all straightforward. How do we go about arranging conditions in which the student would likely be more motivated? Other problematic decisions include:

- What should I teach students in the limited time available?
- How much time should I spend on a particular unit or topic?
- What should I do to help students who are having serious and continuous difficulty learning?

Quite clearly, no decision falls neatly into either category. There is some overlap between them (i.e., a gray area, so to speak). In addition, there are decisions that are straightforward to a point and then become problematic. However, the dichotomy between straightforward and problematic decisions is a useful place to start the discussion of the relationships among assessment, decision making, and evaluation.

Assessment and Straightforward Decisions

If a teacher decides that 94 points earned during a semester results in a grade of "A" being assigned, and if a particular student earns 94 points, then the decision to give the student a grade of "A" is straightforward. (We are, of course, assuming that the 94 points are earned on the basis of reasonably valid, reliable, and objective assessment instruments.) Similarly, suppose a teacher examines the item response summary for a particular commercial mathematics test administered to his or her students. The teacher notices that his or her students do far worse on the computation items than on the concept and problem-solving items. A reasonably straightforward decision may be to spend more time and effort on mathematical computation next year.

Although these decisions are rather straightforward, it is important to note that there is some gray area even in these decisions. In terms of grading, what do you do with a student who earns 93.5 points? Should you round a 93.5 to a 94 (hence, an "A") or is a "miss as good as a mile" (hence, a "B")? What about assigning an A– or a B+? Similarly, with respect to the use of the data from the item response summary, do I want to shift my limited instructional time away from conceptual understanding and problem solving to computation (which is quite reasonable if my desire it to improve student test performance) or do I want to stay the course (because I believe that conceptual understanding and problem solving are far more important than computational accuracy)?

Thus, although these decisions are classified as *straightforward*, they still require some thought. Almost without exception, decisions involve a choice of one alternative over another. The road not taken is not necessarily the wrong road.

Assessment and Problematic Decisions

Calfee and Masuda (1997) suggested that much of classroom assessment is applied social science research. Social science research studies begin with the formulation of questions (Questions) and move to the collection of the data needed to answer the questions (Data Collection). Once data are collected, there is the need to interpret the data so that the questions can be answered (Data Interpretation). Ultimately, there is the "job of deciding what to do with the interpreted findings, the bottom line" (p. 82) (Decision Making). Virtually every problematic decision mentioned earlier requires a research-oriented or inquiry-based approach.

As mentioned earlier, assessment begins when teachers pose *should* questions (Questions). To answer these questions, teachers need information (Data Collection). To reiterate, the type of assessment depends primarily on the nature of information that is needed to answer the question.

Next, teachers must make sense of the information. This is what researchers mean by the phrase *Data Interpretation*. Once teachers make sense of the information they have available to them, they have to decide what to do with it (Decision Making). More specifically, what actions should I take based on the answer to the question I posed? From an assessment perspective, this is, in fact, the bottom line—when the decision is made and resultant actions are planned and implemented.

Often, as in the case of the motivation example, the resultant action is to collect more information. It is important to point out, however, that it is not more of the same information. Rather, the initial question is likely modified based on the initial information, and the new information helps the teacher answer the modified question. The research or inquiry cycle—Question, Data Collection, Data Interpretation, and Decision Making—begins again.

Assessment and Evaluation

Thus far in this initial chapter, we have emphasized purpose, information, and decision making. To restate a previously raised question, "Where does evaluation fit in to all of this?" Evaluation is a specific kind of decision. Specifically, evaluation requires that a judgment be made about the worth or value of something. Typically, evaluative decisions involve the concept of *goodness*—good behavior, good work, and good learning. Interestingly, this trio of goods underlies the traditional elementary school report card. When behavior has been good, the student receives a high mark in Conduct. When work has been good, the student receives a high mark in Effort. Finally, when learning has been good, the student receives a high mark in Achievement.

Evaluation, then, requires some standard (or standards) of goodness. Is Paul's behavior good enough for me to praise it? Is Paula's effort good enough or do I need to get on her about it? Is Paulene's learning good enough to justify a grade of "A?" Performance standards—whether they pertain to conduct, effort, or achievement—are generally responses to the question, "How much is good enough?"

CLOSING COMMENT

Decision making is a critical component of effective teaching. In fact, it may be, as Shavelson (1973) argued, the *basic teaching skill*. Although good information does not necessarily produce wise decisions, having access to good information is certainly an asset for the decision maker. In the remainder of this book, the emphasis is the use of classroom assessment to enable teachers to improve their decision-making capabilities.

CHAPTER TWO

The Why, What, and When of Assessment

In the previous chapter, we discussed the structure of teachers' decisions and the role that assessment does, can, and, in fact, should play in teacher decision making. In this chapter, we address three critical questions concerning assessment as it pertains to teachers' decision making. First, why do teachers assess students? After listing a few obvious answers, we move on to the more interesting ones. Second, what do teachers assess? In chapter 1, it was suggested that teachers base most of their decisions about students on information they gather about the students' classroom behavior, effort, and achievement. In this chapter, we explore each of these in greater detail. Third, when should teachers assess their students? In answering this question, we differentiate between decisions about learning and decisions about teaching, suggesting once again that the timing of assessment depends primarily on the decision being made. This chapter contains three major sections, one dealing with each of these questions.

WHY DO TEACHERS ASSESS STUDENTS?

Teachers assess students for many reasons. They assess because they are required to do so. For example, there are federal-, state-, or district-mandated assessments, such as statewide achievement tests, that must be administered. Teachers also assess their students to justify their decisions. Student: "Why did I get a C–?" Teacher: "Because even though you got a B and a B– on your unit tests (achievement), you didn't turn in any homework (effort)."

From a more positive perspective, one consistent with the message of this book, teachers assess their students to inform the decisions they make about them. "I'm not sure whether to spend more time on this unit. The students seem to be working hard (effort), but they don't seem to be getting it (achievement). And, I have so much more to cover before the end of the year (reality). Well, maybe if I spend a couple more days on it, it will pay dividends in the long run." One of the recurring themes of this book is that informed decisions enable teachers to do their jobs better.

In general, teachers' assessments provide two types of information. Some information allows teachers to **describe** things, whereas other information allows them to begin to offer **explanations** for what they describe. In point of fact, description and explanation are highly related, as a historical example illustrates. Sometime during the 1890s, Alfred Binet (the recognized father of the intelligence test) was commissioned by the French Ministry of Education to devise a test that could be used to differentiate those students who failed in the French education system because they lacked the intellectual capacity from those who failed because they lacked the motivation to succeed. To solve this problem, Binet had to address two issues. First, he had to devise a test that accurately **described** either a student's intellectual capacity or his or her motivation to succeed. Binet opted for the former. Second, he had to **explain** a student's school success or failure in terms of the student's performance on his test. To do this, Binet had to formulate a set of if–then hypotheses. Basically, his argument was as follows:

1. If students score **poorly** on my test and **fail** in school, they are failing because they lack the intellectual capacity to succeed in school.
2. If students score **well** on my test and **fail** in school, they are failing because they lack the motivation to succeed in school.

As we see throughout this chapter and, indeed, throughout the book, teachers, like Binet, can and do use their assessments to describe and explain. Consider motivation, for example. Based on their observations, teachers may **describe** a particular student or entire class as *unmotivated* or *lacking motivation*. Based on this descriptive information, they may raise the question, "What should I do to motivate this unmotivated student (or these unmotivated students)?" To answer this question requires that teachers search for an **explanation** of the student's (or students') lack of motivation. This, in turn, requires teachers to pose and answer a subsequent question: the *why* question. That is, "Why is this student (or why are these students) unmotivated?" Like Binet, teachers must formulate and test hypotheses if they are to answer this question. At least one theoretical framework, referred to as *expectancy x value theory* (Feather, 1982), suggests there are two hypotheses worth investigating:

1. The lack of motivation stems from students' beliefs that education has no value, and, hence, doing well in school is unimportant to them.
2. The lack of motivation stems from students' beliefs that they cannot succeed in school no matter how hard they try.

To determine the reasonableness of each of these hypotheses, teachers must assess (a) the value that students attach to doing well in school, and (b) the beliefs they hold about their ability to be successful in school. The results of this assessment can be summarized a bit simplistically in a four-fold table as shown in Table 2.1.

Three types of motivational problems can be found in Table 2.1. The first is students who value schooling, but do not believe they can succeed in school. The second is students who believe they can succeed in school, but simply do not care to do so because schooling is unimportant to them. The third and clearly the most problematic is students who neither value schooling nor believe they can be successful at it. Each of these types of motivational problems requires a different solution. Although tentative explanations of problems do not solve problems, they do point the direction to potentially useful problem-solving strategies. For example, "Cell B" problems must be solved by finding ways to increase the value students attach to schooling or, perhaps, using incentives or rewards to replace the lack of value they attach to schooling with things they do in fact value. To solve "Cell C" problems, in contrast, we must find ways of convincing students they can be successful in school. A huge part of this convincing, of course, requires students to experience real success. For students who have experienced school failure for several years, this typically means radically different school arrangements (e.g., alternative schools) and/or instructional delivery systems (e.g., technological innovations, tutoring).

The point of this discussion is that description coupled with explanation permits us to engage in a thoughtful, strategic approach to decision making. This is not to suggest that all decisions require both description and explanation. Quite clearly, there are some decisions that rely on description alone. "What grade should I assign to Tom Thompson for this quarter?" "What topics should I emphasize with my class this semester?" "Should I seek advice and counsel about this student from someone with greater knowledge and expertise than I have?" All three of these decisions rely exclusively or primarily on accurate descriptions.

TABLE 2.1
A Framework for Understanding Effort (and Its Lack)

Expectation of Success	Value of Schooling	
	High	Low
High	A	B
Low	C	D

Other decisions, however, require teachers to move beyond description to explanation. "What should I do to help Tom Thompson learn how to solve quadratic equations?" "How should I structure my classroom to minimize disruption and enhance student engagement in learning?" "Where should this child be placed so that his or her needs are more adequately met?" For decisions such as these, description alone does not get us far. Description alone may lead to a fatalistic approach ("He just doesn't care about his schoolwork and there is nothing I can do about it"). It may lead to a random approach ("We've changed teachers three times, put him on restriction more times than I care to admit, and have asked the school counselor to meet with him on a regular basis"). Description alone may lead to an approach that involves treating the symptoms rather than the cause of the problem ("I've asked the teacher to send notes home each time he doesn't turn in his homework"). For these decisions, assessment must provide information that can be used to both describe and explain so that decisions about what should be are more likely to lead to better decisions and, hence, more successful solutions to problems.

WHAT DO TEACHERS ASSESS?

In chapter 1, it was argued that teachers assess classroom behavior, student effort, and student achievement. How do we know this to be true? There are at least three reasons. First, if we examine a typical elementary school report card, particularly those issued to students in Grades 3 through 5 (or 6), we see that students at these grade levels receive separate grades for achievement, conduct (classroom behavior), and work habits (effort). To award these grades, teachers must have some information about how well students do in each of these areas. Second, if we examine research studies that examine what teachers monitor informally as they teach students in classrooms, we see that they focus on what students accomplish (achievement), how well they comply with stated rules and classroom routines (classroom behavior), and the extent to which they are involved in classroom activities and assignments (effort; see e.g., Arlin, 1979; Doyle, 1979a). Third, if we examine research studies that focus on what Doyle (1979b) referred to as the *performance-grade exchange*, we once again encounter the *holy trio*. In simple terms, at some point in their academic careers, students come to grips with the fact that the grades they receive are neither given by the teacher nor earned by them. Rather, they are negotiated. This negotiation involves some combination of ... you guessed it ... how students behave in the classroom, how hard they work, and what they actually learn. So, if I (the student) do not learn as much as you (the teacher) want me to learn, but I am well behaved and I do work (try) hard, then you will give me a slightly higher grade, won't you? Perhaps you will give me a B– (which my parents accept), rather than a C+ (which they will not). In view of the importance of classroom behavior, student effort, and student achievement, then, the remainder of this section of this chapter is given over to a discussion of each of these.

Assessing Student Achievement

Assessing student achievement is no simple matter. Teachers need to make at least two decisions before they engage in this assessment. First, and the topic of this discussion, what should I assess? Second, and the topic of the discussion in chapters 3 and 4, how should I assess it? From a practical point of view, teachers can assess students' knowledge of everything they (teachers) say in class or everything they (students) read in their textbooks.

Consider the previous paragraph, for example. Think of all the assessment tasks that I could write to determine whether you learned what I intended you learn when I wrote it. Here are but three:

- True or false. Assessing student achievement is a simple matter.
- What are the two primary decisions a teacher needs to make prior to engaging in assessment? _____, _____
- Which of these is a topic of discussion in this section of this chapter?
  (a) What should I assess?
  (b) Who should I assess?
  (c) When should I assess?
  (d) Where should I assess?

Given all the available possibilities, how does a teacher determine what should (and should not) be assessed? After all, it is impossible to engage in assessment all the time, and each assessment requires a certain amount of time to complete. Thus, time limitations require that careful choices must be made. Typically, teachers make this determination by deciding what is and is not important. Furthermore, they often make this determination by stating their objectives and communicating these objectives to their students.

What Is an Objective?   In simplest terms, an objective is a statement of what we, as teachers, intend (hope, want, or expect) our students to learn as a result of the instruction we provide them. This definition includes two critical components. First, objectives are stated in terms of our intentions for student learning. Second, as teachers, we believe that we can influence these learning intentions by virtue of our teaching. From a slightly different perspective, objectives give purpose to our students' classroom activities. They help us answer the question, "Why am I asking them to do what I'm asking them to do?"

To clarify matters somewhat, every board game has an objective (typically referred to as the "object of the game"). This objective is found either on the underside of the cover of the box or on a sheet of paper enclosed within it. Some objectives are quite straightforward. The object of *Stratego*, for example, is to "capture the opponent's flag." Similarly, the objective of *Aggravation* is to be the "first player to move all four markers around the board from base to home safe." Other objectives are more complex. The object of *Pictionary*, for example, is to "identify through sketched clues as many words as necessary to advance to the finish square and correctly identify the final word." Similarly, the object of *Scategories* is to "quickly fill out a category list with answers that begin with the same letter. Score points if no other player matches your answers. Score the most points to win the game."

So it is with teachers' objectives. Some are straightforward, whereas others are not. Some are explicitly stated, whereas others are implicit in the activities and materials assigned to students. Some are vague, whereas others are crystal clear. Regardless of their form, however, teachers do have objectives, and their objectives guide (or certainly should guide) their assessment of student achievement.

The Anatomy of an Objective and Analytical Framework.   Like all statements, statements of objective include both nouns and verbs. An analysis of the verbs and nouns used in stating our objectives provides clues as to the achievement expectations we have for our students. Recently, several colleagues and I were involved in the development of a framework that, we believe, enables us to better understand the learning intentions of stated objectives (Anderson et al., 2001).

The framework contains two dimensions (see Table 2.2). The first is derived from the verb of the statement of an objective, whereas the second is derived from the noun. The dimension derived from the verb is referred to as the *cognitive process dimension,* whereas that derived from the noun is labeled the *knowledge dimension.* As shown in Table 2.2, there are six cognitive process categories and four types of knowledge. The task of translating an objective into appropriate assessment tasks, then, begins by analyzing the statement of the objective in terms of the framework. An example of this translation process is shown in Fig. 2.1.

The objective as stated in Fig. 2.1 is, "The student will learn to use the reduce-reuse-recycle approach to conservation." The phrase "the student will learn to" is basically a throw-away phrase in stating objectives. Similar phrases include *the student will be able to* and, more simply, *the student will* (as in, "The student will understand the structure of the periodic table

TABLE 2.2
The Taxonomy Table

The Knowledge Dimension	*The Cognitive Process Dimension*					
	1. Remember	*2. Understand*	*3. Apply*	*4. Analyze*	*5. Evaluate*	*6. Create*
A. Factual						
B. Conceptual						
C. Procedural						
D. Metacognitive						

From, Lorin W. Anderson (Ed.), David R. Krathwohl (Ed.), et al., A taxonomy for learning, teaching, and assessing: A revision of Bloom's taxonomy of educational objectives. Published by Allyn and Bacon, Boston, MA. Copyright © 2001 by Pearson Education. Reprinted with permission of the publisher.

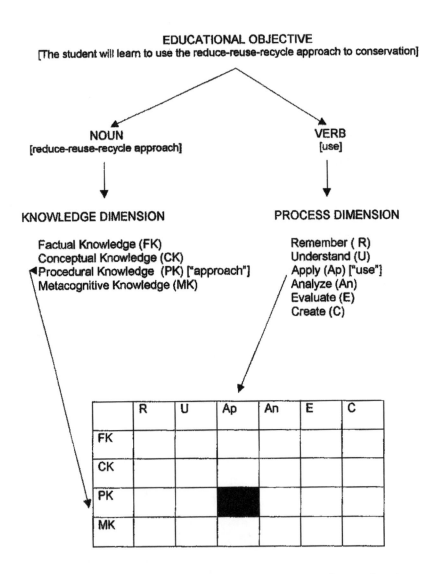

EDUCATIONAL OBJECTIVE
[The student will learn to use the reduce-reuse-recycle approach to conservation]

NOUN
[reduce-reuse-recycle approach]

VERB
[use]

KNOWLEDGE DIMENSION

Factual Knowledge (FK)
Conceptual Knowledge (CK)
◄Procedural Knowledge (PK) ["approach"]
Metacognitive Knowledge (MK)

PROCESS DIMENSION

Remember (R)
Understand (U)
Apply (Ap) ["use"]
Analyze (An)
Evaluate (E)
Create (C)

	R	U	Ap	An	E	C
FK						
CK						
PK			■			
MK						

Note. Objectives are classified in the cells of the Taxonomy Table. The shaded cell in the above table indicates the objective is of the type "*Apply Procedural Knowledge.*"

FIG. 2.1   The journey from an objective to its classification in terms of the Taxonomy Table. Published by Allyn and Bacon, Boston, MA. Copyright © 2001 by Pearson Education. Reprinted with permission of the publisher.

of the elements"). Furthermore, *will* can be replaced by *should* or *is expected to* without changing the meaning of the objective at all. In the reduce-reuse-recycle, example, however, the verb that is important in terms of our expectations of student learning is *use*. What is the student supposed to learn to use? The answer is "the reduce-reuse-recycle approach to conservation." This is the noun (or, more precisely, noun phrase).

Having identified the verb and noun, we examine each in terms of the rows and columns of the Taxonomy Table. *Use* is another word for *apply*. An approach is a procedure. Thus, "The student will learn to use the reduce-reuse-recycle approach to conversation" is an objective of the type, Apply Procedural Knowledge.

To simplify this translation process, we prepared two additional tables. The first table contains a listing of the verbs often found in statements of objectives (Table 2.3). These verbs are organized into the six cognitive process categories. Thus, we see that recognize, identify, recall, and retrieve are all related to Remember. As shown in Table 2.3, *use* is indeed associated with Apply. Similarly, the second table contains a list of examples within each of the four knowledge categories (Table 2.4). Although *approach* is not specifically mentioned in Table 2.4, approaches are indeed similar to skills, algorithms, techniques, and, particularly, methods.

To see how Table 2.3 and Table 2.4 can aid in the transition process, consider the following objective: "The student should be able to compare and contrast shared powers and parliamentary systems as a means of organizing constitutional governments." We begin with the identification of the relevant verb(s). *The student should be able to* is the throw-away phrase. Having removed it, we see there are two verbs: *compare* and *contrast*. Examining Table 2.3, we see that compare and contrast are both linked with Understand. The relevant noun phrase is *shared powers and parliamentary systems*. (The closing phrase simply reminds us that there are two ways (means) of organizing constitutional governments.) *Shared powers* and *parliamentary systems* are types of constitutional governments. Because *types* are categories and classifications, *shared powers* and *parliamentary systems* are both examples of Conceptual Knowledge (see Table 2.4). Our analysis of this objective, then, leads us to believe that the aforementioned objective is of the type Understand Conceptual Knowledge.

Using the Framework to Assess Student Achievement.   At this point, you may be saying to yourself, "I see how the Taxonomy Table can help me make sense of my objectives. But how does this help me engage in better assessment of student achievement?" The answer is straightforward: Consider the Taxonomy Table a labor-saving device. An analysis of the published standards in five states led me to the conclusion that the vast majority of these standards (with *standards* being simply a modern-day word for

TABLE 2.3
Cognitive Processes

CATEGORIES & COGNITIVE PROCESSES	ALTERNATIVE NAMES	DEFINITIONS AND EXAMPLES
1. REMEMBER-Retrieve relevant knowledge from long-term memory		
1.1 RECOGNIZING	Identifying	Locating knowledge in long-term memory that is consistent with presented material (e.g., Recognize the dates of important events in U.S. history)
1.2 RECALLING	Retrieving	Retrieving relevant knowledge from long-term memory (e.g., Recall the dates of important events in U.S. history)
2. UNDERSTAND-Construct meaning from instructional messages, including oral, written, and graphic communication		
2.1 INTERPRETING	Clarifying, paraphrasing, representing, translating	Changing from one form of representation (e.g., numerical) to another (e.g., verbal) (e.g., Paraphrase important speeches and documents)
2.2 EXEMPLIFYING	Illustrating, instantiating	Finding a specific example or illustration of a concept or principle (e.g., Give examples of various artistic painting styles)
2.3 CLASSIFYING	Categorizing, subsuming	Determining that something belongs to a category (e.g., Classify observed or described cases of mental disorders)
2.4 SUMMARIZING	Abstracting, generalizing	Abstracting a general theme or major point(s) (e.g., Write a short summary of the event portrayed on a videotape)
2.5 INFERRING	Concluding, extrapolating, interpolating, predicting	Drawing a logical conclusion from presented information (e.g., In learning a foreign language, infer grammatical principles from examples)
2.6 COMPARING	Contrasting, mapping, matching	Detecting correspondences between two ideas, objects, and the like (e.g., Compare historical events to contemporary situations)
2.7 EXPLAINING	Constructing models	Constructing a cause-and-effect model of a system (e.g., Explain the cause of important 18th Century events in France)
3. APPLY-Carry out or use a procedure in a given situation		
3.1 EXECUTING	Carrying out	Applying a procedure to a familiar task (e.g., Divide one whole number by another whole number, both with multiple digits)
3.2 IMPLEMENTING	Using	Applying a procedure to an unfamiliar task (e.g., Use Newton's Second Law in situations in which it is appropriate)

4. ANALYZE-Break material into its constituent parts and determine how the parts relate to one another and to an overall structure or purpose		
4.1 DIFFERENTIATING	Discriminating, distinguishing, focusing, selecting	Distinguishing relevant from irrelevant parts or important from unimportant parts of presented material (e.g., Distinguish between relevant and irrelevant numbers in a mathematical word problem)
4.2 ORGANIZING	Finding coherence, integrating, outlining, parsing, structuring	Determining how elements fit or function within a structure (e.g., Structure evidence in a historical description into evidence for and against a particular historical explanation)
4.3 ATTRIBUTING	Deconstructing	Determine a point of view, bias, values, or intent underlying presented material (e.g., Determine the point of view of the author of an essay in terms of his or her political perspective)
5. EVALUATE-Make judgments based on criteria and standards		
5.1 CHECKING	Coordinating, detecting, monitoring, testing	Detecting inconsistencies of fallacies within a process or product; determining whether a process or product has internal consistency; detecting the effectiveness of a procedure as it is being implemented (e.g., Determine if a scientist's conclusions follow from observed data)
5.2 CRITIQUING	Judging	Detecting inconsistencies between a product and external criteria, determining whether a product has external consistency; detecting the appropriateness of a procedure for a given problem (e.g., Judge which of two methods is the best way to solve a given problem)
6. CREATE-Put elements together to form a coherent or functional whole; reorganize elements into a new patter or structure		
6.1 GENERATING	Hypothesizing	Coming up with alternative hypotheses based on criteria (e.g., Generate hypotheses to account for an observed phenomenon)
6.2 PLANNING	Designing	Devising a procedure for accomplishing some task (e.g., Plan a research paper on a given historical topic)
6.3 PRODUCING	Constructing	Inventing a product (e.g., Build habitats for a specific purpose)

Published by Allyn and Bacon, Boston, MA. Copyright © 2001 by Pearson Education. Reprinted with permission of the publisher.

TABLE 2.4
Types of Knowledge

MAJOR TYPES AND SUBTYPES	EXAMPLES
A. FACTUAL KNOWLEDGE-The basic elements students must know to be acquainted with discipline or solve problems in it	
Aa. Knowledge of terminology	Technical vocabulary, music symbols
Ab. Knowledge of specific details and elements	Major natural resources, reliable sources of information
B. CONCEPTUAL KNOWLEDGE-The interrelationships among the basic elements withing a larger structure that enable them to function together	
Ba. Knowledge of classifications and categories	Periods of geological time, forms of business ownership
Bb. Knowledge of principles and generalizations	Pythagorean theorem, law of supply and demand
Bc. Knowledge of theories, models, and structures	Theory of evolution, structure of Congress
C. PROCEDURAL KNOWLEDGE-How to do something, methods of inquiry, and criteria for using skills, algorithms, techniques, and methods	
Ca. Knowledge of subject-specific skills and algorithms	Skills used in painting with water colors, whole-number division algorithm
Cb. Knowledge of subject-specific techniques and methods	Interviewing techniques, scientific method
Cc. Knowledge of criteria for determining when to use appropriate procedures	Criteria used to determine when to apply a procedure involving Newton's second law, criteria used to judge the feasibility of using a particular method to estimate business costs
D. METACOGNITIVE KNOWLEDGE-Knowledge of cognition in general as well as awareness and knowledge of one's own cognition	
Da. Strategic knowledge	Knowledge of outlining as a means of capturing the structure of a unit of subject matter in a text book, knowledge of the use of heuristics
Db. Knowledge about cognitive tasks, including appropriate contextual and conditional knowledge	Knowledge of the types of test particular teachers administer, knowledge of the cognitive demands of different tasks
Dc. Self-knowledge	Knowledge that critiquing essays is a personal strength, whereas writing essays is a personal weakness; awareness of one's own knowledge level

mandated *objectives*) can be placed into one of three cells of the Taxonomy Table (Anderson et al., 2001). Based on these existing state standards, we want or expect our students to: (a) remember factual knowledge, (b) understand conceptual knowledge, and (c) apply procedural knowledge (see Table 2.5).

One of the keys to better assessment of student achievement, then, is to develop or locate prototypical ways of assessing objectives that fall within these three cells.

For example, to assess an objective of the type Remember Factual Knowledge, one can follow a simple procedure. First, state the factual knowledge to be recalled. Second, transform the statement into a question. Third, have students either supply or select an answer to the question. How does this procedure look in practice?

- O. Henry was known as the "father of the short story."
- Who was known as the "father of the short story?"
- _____ or (a) Poe, (b) Tennyson, (c) O. Henry, (d) Irving.

Similarly, to assess an objective of the type Understand Conceptual Knowledge, the following task format serves us well: "Which of these is an example of X?" (where X is the label for the concept of importance). This question would be followed by, say, four choices, one of which is a correct example. This results in questions such as these:

Which of these is an example of a true spider?
Which of these is an example of iambic pentameter?
Which of these is an example of a rational number?
Which of these is an example of an impressionistic painting?

Each question would be followed by four plausible response options that are homogeneous (i.e., they belong to the same general category of response options).

Finally, to assess an objective of the type Apply Procedural Knowledge, the following three-step procedure is quite useful. First, provide students with information about some problem or situation. Second, ask students to use specific procedural knowledge to solve the problem or find an answer to a question. Third, either have students write the solution or answer or have them select a solution or answer from among alternatives. How does this look in practice? Tables 2.6 and 2.7 provide two examples, the first using a selection task format and the second using a performance task format.

Quite clearly, these prototypes are not the only prototypes appropriate for these three primary cells of the Taxonomy Table. Rather, they are meant

TABLE 2.5
Most Frequent Cells

The Cognitive Process Dimension

The Knowledge Dimension	1. Remember	2. Understand	3. Apply	4. Analyze	5. Evaluate	6. Create
A. Factual	▭					
B. Conceptual		▭				
C. Procedural			▭			
D. Metacognitive						

TABLE 2.6
Sample Assessment Task For Apply Procedural Knowledge

Consider the information presented in the following chart. Use the division algorithm to calculate the cost per ounce of "rich chunky peanut butter." In arriving at your answer, pay particular attention to the units of measurement.

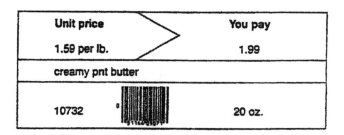

What of these is the cost per ounce of "rich chunky peanut butter?"

(a) 8 cents

(b) 10 cents

(c) 12 cents

(d) 20 cents

TABLE 2.7

Sample Assessment Task for Apply Procedural Knowledge

Suppose the density of a material is 2.5 pounds per cubic inch. Further, suppose its mass is 17.5 pounds. What is the volume of the material? Show your work using the formula $D = M/V$.

Step 1.

Step 2.

Step 3.

Step 4.

to be illustrative, not exhaustive, of the various possibilities that exist. The point, however, is that the Taxonomy Table not only helps teachers understand objectives. It also helps them design appropriate assessment tasks in a reasonably efficient manner.

Before moving to the next section, two additional points must be made clear. First, by saying that the majority of current standards and objectives **do fall** within one of these three cells does not mean that the majority of current standards and objectives **should fall** within one of these three cells. At the same time, however, our assessments, to be valid, must assess what **is**, not what **should be**. The authors of some classroom assessment books offer the following advice: Avoid having all multiple-choice items test rote memorization. This simply is poor advice. If all objectives pertain to rote memorization, then all assessment tasks should do likewise. The fact that students may experience a steady diet of rote memorization is a curriculum problem, not an assessment one.

Second, prototypical assessment tasks can and perhaps should be developed for all 24 cells of the Taxonomy Table. Yet from a validity as well as an efficiency point of view, that development should begin with those cells into which the majority of objectives actually fall. We discuss the assessment of student achievement in greater detail in chapters 3 and 4.

Assessing Student Effort

As Doyle (1986) wrote almost two decades ago, "Students' academic work in school is defined by the academic tasks that are embedded in the [curriculum] they encounter daily.... Students will learn what a task leads them to do, that is, they will acquire information and operations that are necessary to accomplish the tasks they encounter" (p. 177). To paraphrase Doyle, academic tasks give purpose and meaning to what students think, do, and, perhaps, even feel in the classroom.

Academic tasks are so ingrained in classrooms that we often fail to notice them. To refresh your memory, here are just a few (with italics used to emphasize the task being assigned to the students):

- "I'm going to read you a story. When I finish I want you to *list the two major reasons that Freddy ran away from home.*"
- "Turn to page 129 and look at the diagram of the electrical circuit. This electric circuit will not work. *Examine the diagram, identify the problem, and tell what you would do to fix the problem so that it will work.* You will have about 10 minutes."
- "I've written five problems on the board. Let's see ... Allyson, Philip, Arturo, Jane, and Fritz ... go to the board. I want each of you to *work*

one of the problems. Those of you still at your seats, I want you to *watch them carefully and see if they make any mistakes.*"

- "Yesterday, we were discussing the bones in the human arm. Who can *show me where the humorous bone is located?* [pause] Cassandra?"

Doyle identified three types of academic tasks: memory, comprehension, and procedural. The reader should note the clear and explicit connection between Doyle's tasks and the three most frequently encountered types of objectives mentioned earlier: memory tasks→recalling factual knowledge; comprehension tasks→understanding conceptual knowledge; and procedural tasks→applying procedural knowledge. (Note. The arrows indicate that each particular type of task facilitates the achievement of each particular type of objective.)

Assigning a task is a signal to students that they are supposed to get to work. More specifically, they are expected to put forth the effort needed to accomplish the task—to get the work done. Thus, tasks link students with objectives by means of the effort that students expend on the tasks. That is, no effort, no achievement.

Effort is a far more complex concept than it appears on the surface, being composed of at least three different facets. First, there is the amount of effort. Second, there is the quality of effort. Third, there is the reason for expending the effort (or, more often, not expending the necessary effort).

Assessing Amount of Effort. As teachers monitor students as they work on various tasks, they gather observational data. Quite quickly, they notice which students are on task and which are not. They may also notice which students work continuously and which work more sporadically. If they are particularly astute, they may notice which students stay on task when difficulties arise (i.e., they persevere) and which stop working at that point and start looking around for help.

Continuous effort and, particularly, perseverance lead to the connection between effort and motivation made by both academics and teachers. For example, Carroll (1985) defined *perseverance* as the amount of time a student was willing to spend in learning. Perseverance, in turn, was a function of "what is ordinarily called 'motivation' or desire to learn" (p. 67). Hence, students who show a "marked willingness to spend time, beyond the ordinary schedule, in a given task," a "willingness to withstand discomfort" when working on a given task, or "willingness to face failure" (p. 66) are all said to be highly motivated.

Similarly, teachers routinely link a student's effort with his or her motivation. Students who are highly distractible, students who do not turn in homework, and students who wander aimlessly around the room are all said to lack motivation. All of these inferences are made based on teacher observations. Hence, observational assessment is the primary means to assess the amount of student effort.

Assessing Quality of Effort.   Two students may spend exactly the same amount of time working on a task, yet one completes the task more quickly, to a higher level, or both. What accounts for this difference? One possible answer is that the students differ in the quality of their effort. What is quality of effort? Consider the following example.

Ms. Milani sends Anthony and Arthur to the library to gather information on arthropods and tells them to return to the classroom with their findings in 30 minutes. Anthony goes to the dictionary and looks up the definition of *arthropod*. Next, he goes to the card catalog and looks up arthropod, locating two books—one on crustaceans, the other on arachnids. He wanders through the bookshelves and is unable to find either book. He goes to the librarian and asks about the books. The librarian looks on the computer and finds that both are checked out. Anthony returns to the dictionary, takes a piece of paper out of his pocket, and copies the definition of *arthropod*. Seeing that his 30 minutes is up, he returns to the classroom.

Realizing that he only has 30 minutes, Arthur goes directly to the *Encyclopedia Brittanica*. As he reads about arthropods, he begins to draw a tree diagram with arthropods on the top, followed by crustaceans, arachnids, and insects, followed by examples of each. He goes to the librarian and asks if he can make overhead transparencies of several of the pictures in the encyclopedia. The librarian says, "Yes." Arthur makes three transparencies and heads back to the classroom.

Both students worked on the assignment the entire 30 minutes. Neither was ever off task. Quite clearly, however, Arthur's effort was of higher quality. This difference in the quality of effort, not in the amount of effort, resulted in a substantial difference in the quality of their product.

How do we assess quality of effort? Certainly, observational methods can be used. However, the use of these methods would involve shadowing the students (as we did in the prior examples). Thus, in most situations, observational methods are not a practical means to gather information about the quality of student effort. Rather, we must rely on student self-reports. These self-reports may be in the form of time logs or questionnaires.

One promising area of research related to quality of effort deals with metacognition, particularly what has been termed *self-regulated learning* (Boekaerts, Pintrich, & Zeidner, 2001). Stated simply, self-regulated learners plan, organize, self-instruct, and self-evaluate at various stages of the learning process. All of these activities—planning, organizing, instructing, and evaluating—are likely to result in a higher quality of effort being put forth by students. In recent years, several instruments related to self-regulated learning have been developed. We review some of these briefly in chapter 5.

Assessing Reasons for Lack of Effort.   Here is another place at which motivation enters the discussion. A good place to start is to return to Carroll's (1985) discussion of perseverance. Carroll pointed out there are many reasons for being willing to spend time learning: "to please the teacher, to please one's parents or friends, to get good grades or other external reward, to achieve self-confidence in one's learning ability, to feed one's self-esteem, to avoid disapproval" (p. 67). Similarly, there are numerous reasons for not being willing to spend time learning. They include: "to avoid the responsibilities which learning brings, to avoid the exertion of learning, to behave consistently with one's image of oneself as a non-learner, or to avoid wasting time on learning tasks of no perceived importance" (p. 67).

Carroll, then, moved the discussion to a concern for why students are or are not motivated, with the *why* question being asked more frequently when effort is lacking than when it is present. It is in this context that concerns for intrinsic and extrinsic motivation arise. Is the student putting forth the necessary effort because of love of learning (an intrinsic motivating factor)? Is the student putting forth the necessary effort to please his or her parents (an extrinsic motivating factor)?

The expectancy-value theory (mentioned earlier) is another attempt to answer the why of student effort. There are two important aspects of this theory as it pertains to student achievement, both of which were mentioned in chapter 1. First, students must value either what they are expected to achieve (the objectives) or the rewards attached to the achievement per se (e.g., grades, status, parental pride). Second, students must believe they can achieve what they are expected to achieve. This is where expectancy enters in to the equation; there must be an expectancy of success. For students to believe that they can learn what they are expected to learn, they must see some connection between their effort and their achievement. Unfortunately, the strength of the effort–achievement connection decreases the longer students are in school (Stipek, 1986). Over time, effort is replaced with ability (a lot or little), luck (good or bad), task difficulty (easy or difficult), or influence of other people (good teacher or poor teacher). An increasing number of students begin to believe that no amount of effort will lead to academic success, and they begin to show evidence of learned helplessness. *Can't* becomes a key word in their vocabulary. Once there is a disconnect between effort and achievement, it becomes far more difficult to motivate students.

In assessing the reasons for the lack of effort on the part of students, we once again must reply on student self-reports. These particular self-reports move us into what traditionally has been known as the *affective domain* and *affective assessment*. More is said about affective assessment in chapter 5.

Assessing Classroom Behavior

In many respects, teachers' classrooms are their castles. Teachers are not particularly happy if they have to share their classrooms with other teachers, and they are very unhappy if they have to move from classroom to classroom throughout the day without a classroom of their own. At the same time, however, teachers expect relatively little of the students who inhabit their classrooms. Simply stated, they expect students to (a) comply with established rules and regulations, and (b) get along with others. To teachers (and to most sane people), these do not seem to be unreasonable requests.

Unfortunately, however, nothing that appears to be so simple is, in fact, that simple. Researchers have spent countless hours studying various types and aspects of students' classroom behaviors. They have addressed compliance, cooperation, prosocial behaviors, disruption, and aggression. All of these have been encompassed within the general term, *misbehavior*. Yet, each of these terms has a different meaning—a different emphasis. Compliance focuses on the first expectation, whereas prosocial behaviors focus on the second. Cooperation can refer to either the first expectation (as in cooperation with teacher requests or demands) or the second expectation (as in cooperation with fellow students). Disruption is said to occur when students not only fail to comply with classroom rules and regulations, but also interfere with classroom instruction. That is, they engage in behaviors that cause the teacher to stop teaching and address the behavior per se. Finally, aggression occurs when the behavior exhibited by a student is intended to harm other students or the teacher (omitting from the discussion self-directed aggression).

Lack of compliance, lack of cooperation, and absence of prosocial behaviors may or may not be ignored by the teacher depending on his or her level of tolerance for such behavior. In contrast, aggressive behaviors must be addressed. Whether ignored or addressed, however, all of these behaviors must be assessed. How do/should teachers assess the classroom behaviors of their students? The clear-cut answer to this question is that they do so by means of observation.

Students' classroom behaviors are generally assessed informally. That is, teachers monitor classroom behaviors somewhat tacitly until some type of negative behavior is observed. In contrast to classroom researchers, teachers typically do not use structured observation forms to record students' classroom behaviors. When negative behaviors are observed, all of this changes. At this point, teachers become more like classroom researchers. They know, either explicitly or implicitly, that they might have to document the negative behavior, particularly in the case of disruptive or aggressive behavior that leads to a recommendation of some form of formal discipline. Documentation means that generality must give way to specificity; generalities must be replaced with specific behaviors.

Like all assessment, the assessment of classroom behavior can provide both descriptive and explanatory information. Based on the available information, we know something about how one student behaves or how one class of students behaves (i.e., we can describe the behavior). Unfortunately, we do not know why he, she, or they behave they way they do (i.e., we cannot explain the behavior). Attempting to explain why a particular student engages in a particular behavior often requires other people to be brought into the discussion. When teachers should seek outside assistance or refer students for additional assessment and/or assistance is addressed in chapter 7. In contrast, attempting to explain why large numbers of students (perhaps an entire class) behave in a certain way often leads us to examine ourselves. As teachers, what are we doing to cause, effect, or otherwise influence the behavior of our students? If we are as "dull as dirt," can we truly expect our students to do anything other than fall asleep? If we fail to intervene properly in early skirmishes, do we really believe that the skirmish will not escalate?

The assessment of classroom behavior typically involves some form of observation, informal or systematic. In contrast, explanations of the causes of misbehavior generally require both (a) information from self-reports of students, and (b) a causal model that allows us to link the self-report information with the misbehavior. Both of these issues are addressed in chapter 5.

WHEN SHOULD TEACHERS ASSESS STUDENTS?

A somewhat cavalier, but quite honest, answer to this question is that teachers should assess students when they need information to make decisions about them. That is, there should be a clear connection between the timing of an assessment and the decision-making process. Unfortunately, however, this is not always possible. The timing of some assessments is mandated. State achievement tests, for example, are administered when state bureaucrats say they are to be administered. Bad timing is unfortunate because it quite likely results in a disconnect between assessment and decision making, particularly decisions concerning individual students.

Most state achievement tests are administered in the spring. The completed tests are then sent away to be scored. Preliminary results are returned to the school districts in the summer and final results in the fall. Between the spring test administration and the fall appearance of test results, most students have changed classes (i.e., they are with a different group of students) and have moved up a grade in the school system. This produces several problems. First, the class-level report generally does not match the current class membership. Thus, instructional decisions, which typically require some form of data aggregation, are difficult to make. If instructional decisions are made, they must be made rather cautiously because the data are a bit dated (e.g., from April to October). On an individual student basis, the data cannot be used to grade students or make promotion/retention decisions because final grades have already been assigned to the students and students have already been promoted or retained. Although there are some decisions that can be made based on these state achievement test results, many decisions are preempted because of the timing of the assessment relative to the timing of the decision.

In these final sections of this chapter, we briefly examine two categories of decisions. They are decisions about learning and decisions about teaching.

Decisions About Learning

We begin this discussion by differentiating learning from achievement. *Achievement* is what or how much a student has learned by some point in time (e.g., the end of a unit, the end of term). *Learning*, in contrast, is what or how much a student has learned over time (e.g., from the beginning to the end of the unit, from the beginning to the end of a term). Decisions about learning require teachers to obtain information about student achievement at multiple points in time. Traditionally, learning is assessed by administering the same achievement test at the beginning and end of some period of time (e.g., unit, term). The difference between the pre- and posttest scores is taken as a measure of learning. This approach to assessing learning, although still viable, is rarely used in practice.

An approach to assessing learning that is being seen more frequently is the use of portfolios. As Smith, Smith, and DeLisi (2001) pointed out, portfolios are not new. They argued that, in the past, portfolios were called *folders,* and they were where students kept their work. There are important differences between folders and portfolios, however. One important difference is that portfolios are generally more organized than folders. In this regard, Gallagher (1998) defined a *portfolio* as an "organized collection of student products and recorded performances" (p. 241).

To assess learning rather than achievement, however, another phrase must be added to the definition: over time. In this regard, Airasian (1997) placed portfolios in their proper context. "Portfolios are more than folders that hold all of a pupil's work. They contain a consciously selected sample [of work] that is intended to show growth and development toward some important curriculum goal" (p. 239).

How are achievement and learning related to the issue of when to assess students? If decisions are to be based on achievement, then the information should be collected as near to the decision as possible (e.g., final examinations are administered in close proximity to end-of-term grades).

However, if decisions are to be based on learning, then a plan for information collection over time must be developed and implemented.

Decisions About Teaching

To keep things simple (yet not overly simplistic), we differentiate curriculum from instruction as follows. *Curriculum* is primarily concerned with **what** we teach, whereas *instruction* is primarily concerned with **how** we teach it. The primary curriculum question is, "Are we teaching the right things?" In contrast, the primary instructional question is, "Are we teaching things in the right way?" Although more is said about decisions about curriculum and instruction in chapter 7, there are a few issues that are addressed here concerning the timing of assessments.

Instructional decisions may be informed by information collected at three general points in time: before, during, and after. Prior to instruction (e.g., at the beginning of a term or year), teachers may use questionnaires to collect a variety of information about students' interests, values, self-esteem, preferred learning environments, and the like. Prior to instruction, teachers may also peruse students' permanent files to get some overall idea of his or her students. Airasian (1997) referred to these prior-to-instruction assessments as *sizing up* assessments. These assessments provide information about the class as a whole as well as about individual students. Are there some common interests I can use to design or select high-interest materials? Who are the students that are likely to need more of my attention and assistance? These are examples of the questions that teachers can answer using information obtained from their sizing up assessments.

During instruction, teachers can use information obtained from observations and student performance on various assessment tasks to make mid-course corrections. The use of information in this way is referred to as *formative assessment* (Airasian, 1997; Smith, Smith, & DeLisi, 2001) because it both informs the teacher and forms the basis for making changes in the delivery of instruction. It is during instruction that the blending of learning tasks and assessment tasks, mentioned in chapter 1, is the greatest. For example, students may be given a writing assignment in which they are to take and defend a position on an issue (e.g., capital punishment) that would be consistent with the philosophy or point of view of particular historical or contemporary individuals. As the students are engaged in writing, the teacher circulates around the room, stopping to check progress and providing encouragement and other forms of assistance as needed. Suppose that, during this monitoring, the teacher notices several students are giving the right position on the issue, but are offering the wrong reasons for taking the position. Does the teacher continue the one-on-one supervision, or does the teacher reconvene the class as a whole in an attempt to correct the misunderstanding? This is the type of instructional decision that is made on the basis on during instruction assessment.

Finally, there are a variety of decisions to be made after instruction has been completed. These decisions are based on what has been termed *summative assessment* (Airasian, 1997; Gredler, 1999) because the information is intended to sum up what has been learned to that point in time presumably as a result of the instruction provided. The primary use of these summative assessments is to assign grades to students. However, one can imagine circumstances in which these assessments serve a formative function. For example, suppose that the results of a summative assessment indicate that over one half of the students failed to achieve the unit objectives. As the teacher, do you move on to the next unit anyway because of a need (real or perceived) to move on so that all of the material can be covered by the end of the year? Or do you decide to use the results of the summative assessment to identify those objectives on which fairly large numbers of students are having difficulty learning and spend 2 or 3 more days on those objectives? If you choose the latter, your summative assessment is functioning as a formative one.

So far in this section, we have focused exclusively on instructional decisions. We end this section (and this chapter) with two examples of curricular decisions. Early in my career, I worked with a group of elementary school teachers one summer to help them develop curriculum units as part of a federally funded Title IV-C project. In addition to specific objectives, curricular materials, and instructional activities, each unit had to include a multiple-choice test to be used as both a pretest and posttest, with the difference used as evidence of the unit's effectiveness. About 2 weeks after school started, I visited the school and talked to some of teachers about their initial units. One teacher reluctantly showed me the results of her unit pretest. About 80% of the students had achieved the preset mastery performance standard. Naively I asked, "So what did you do?" She responded, "I taught the unit anyway. Wasn't I supposed to?"

I learned two things from that experience. First, many teachers live in fear of not doing what they are supposed to do. For these teachers, using assessment information to make defensible curriculum decisions is a difficult proposition indeed. Second, it is difficult to expect teachers to make in-flight curricular decisions. What are they going to do with all the materials and activities they have prepared? With what are they going to replace the unit if they skip it?

My second example comes from an experience I had several months ago. Once again I was working with a group of teachers on curriculum development. This time it involved elementary school and middle school teachers working during the summer, with an emphasis on a modified project-based approach to curriculum design. That is, each unit would be defined, in part, by a culminating project that students would complete. The teachers were to come up with project requirement and scoring rubrics for each of their seven or eight identified units.

After two or three of these were developed at each grade level, two district-level administrators and I met to review them. In general, they were quite good, but there was one obvious problem. Namely, the project requirements developed by the sixth-grade teachers (beginning of middle school) were notably less demanding academically than those developed by the fifth-grade teachers (end of elementary school). The sixth-grade projects involved designing posters and preparing pop-up books, whereas the fifth-grade projects involved comparison–contrast essays and research reports.

Rather than confront the sixth-grade teachers, we decided to share all of the projects with all of the teachers. The projects then became the assessments. Very quickly, the sixth-grade teachers saw the problem. There projects were much more like those given to third- and fourth-grade students than those given to seventh- and eighth-grade students. Based on this newly acquired information, modifications in the sixth-grade projects were made. Furthermore, the understanding they gained from the information translated into more demanding projects being developed for subsequent units.

What does this example have to do with the timing of assessment? It reinforces my belief that curricular decisions are best made away from the business of teaching. Unlike instructional decisions that can and should be made before, during, and after, curricular decisions should be made outside of school as much as possible. By *outside*, I mean two things. First, and clearly from a timing perspective, curriculum work done during the summer months is much preferable to work done during the school year. Second, work done in a venue different from the school is more likely to be productive and yield more creative, substantive results. Perhaps teachers need to meet *outside the box* to think *outside the box*.

CLOSING COMMENT

Before deciding how to assess students, teachers must determine the purpose of the assessment, the assessment information that is needed to accomplish the purpose, and the timing of the assessment. The primary purpose of assessment is to gather the information teachers need to make sound, defensible decisions. To make these decisions, teachers may need to describe students' behavior, effort, and/or achievement. In many cases, however, teachers need to explain the behavior, effort, and/or achievement. If done well, assessment provides information that can be used to make a variety of decisions—decisions that can substantially improve a teacher's effectiveness in working with his or her students.

CHAPTER THREE

Assessing Achievement Using Selection and Short-Answer Tasks

The purpose of this chapter is to describe a 10-step procedure for designing instruments to assess student achievement—a procedure that, with some minor modifications, is applicable to all types of assessment task formats. The procedure is outlined in Table 3.1. In this chapter, the focus is on assessment instruments that contain selection and short-answer tasks. In chapter 4, the focus is assessment instruments that contain performance and extended response tasks.

TABLE 3.1
Procedure for Designing Instruments to Assess Student Achievement

1. Decide on your most important unit objectives and use the Taxonomy Table to determine the appropriate cell or cells for each objective.

2. Determine the length of the unit assessment.

3. Based on your understanding of the objective in terms of the Taxonomy Table, select or write several assessment tasks for each objective.

4. Have your assessment tasks reviewed by someone else; make changes as necessary.

5. Prepare unit assessment.

6. Prepare method of scoring student responses.

7. Administer unit assessment.

8. Analyze results of unit assessment.

9. Assign student scores on unit assessment.

10. Place assessment instrument, the results of your analysis, and students' scores in a file folder.

STEP 1: DECIDE ON MOST IMPORTANT OBJECTIVES

We begin with two fundamental and complementary propositions. First, you cannot assess everything. Second, not everything is worth assessing. As a consequence, the first step in designing an instrument to assess student achievement is to determine what is worth assessing. To make this determination teachers would be wise to focus on what may be termed a *curriculum unit* or *unit of instruction*. Whatever terminology is used, a unit is a series of lessons related to a single topic or cluster of objectives. Typically, units require from 2 to 3 weeks to complete (although some are longer).

Units have titles that tell us something about what the unit is about. For example, we may see a unit on "Exploring Word Origins" in elementary language arts, a unit on "Fractions, Decimals, and Percents" in middle-school mathematics, and a unit on "The Media and Politics" in high school social studies. In a textbook-oriented curriculum, units often correspond with chapters of textbooks, although when this is the case, the units may be slightly shorter (from 5 to 8 days). Within the context of each unit, there is a fundamental question that must be addressed by teachers. Of all the things students could learn in this unit, what are the most important? The answers to this question become the unit objectives. Determining unit objectives, then, is a matter of setting priorities.

For many teachers, this is a difficult question to answer because the answer depends on their values. Is learning about history more important than learning how historians study history? Is learning to write in a formal way more important than learning to write creatively? Is learning to think for yourself more important than learning what others have thought? It might be nice to teach all of these things. Unfortunately, there is just so much time. Consequently, regardless of whether they want to, teachers address these questions either implicitly or explicitly. As mentioned above, their answers to these questions either become or inform their objectives.

Increasingly, teachers are having this difficult value question answered for them by state legislators, state departments of education, and/or school district administrators. Grade-level objectives (termed *standards*) for most academic disciplines or subject matters have been established in most states. Even when they are given state standards, however, teachers must still organize and sequence units (because they cannot teach them all at the same time). Furthermore, some of the state standards are quite broad—one might say vague. In this case, unit objectives provide clarity and direction to the state standards.

STEP 2: DETERMINE THE LENGTH OF THE UNIT ASSESSMENT(S)

From an assessment point of view, teachers need to address a second, related question. On how many of these objectives should student achievement be assessed? The answer to this question depends, in turn, on answers to two more questions. First, how much time does the teacher want to devote to assessment? Second, does the teacher want to get reliable information about student achievement with respect to **each** assessed objective, or is it sufficient to get reliable information about student achievement relative to the assessed objectives **collectively**?

Time Spent on Assessment

Consider a 3-week unit, where each of the 15 lessons or class periods lasts 50 minutes. Therefore, 750 minutes are spent on the unit. Suppose a teacher decides to devote two lessons or class periods to assessment. Therefore, 100 minutes (or slightly more than one eighth of the total time allocated to the unit) are spent on assessment. Is this reasonable? Is it too much? Is it too little? For most, if not all, teachers, these are difficult questions to answer. Certainly, no teacher wants to spend half the time on assessment and, I would suspect, few teachers would want to spend even as much as one fourth of the time on assessment. At the same time, however, few, if any, teachers would spend no time at all on assessment. Within these boundaries, somewhere around one eighth of the time spent on assessment seems reasonable. For some teachers, this may be a bit high; for others, this may be a bit low. Yet, this is the type of judgment that teachers make all the time.

If a teacher decides to devote two class periods to assessment, how many assessment tasks can be included on the assessment instrument(s)? The answer to this question depends on the type(s) of assessment tasks to be written. If selection and/or short-answer tasks are used, a rule of thumb is to begin with as many assessment tasks as there are minutes devoted to assessment. Adjustments can then be made based on factors such as the age of the students, the complexity of the objectives, the difficulty of the tasks, and so on. When assessing third-grade students' recall of their multiplication facts, for example, it is reasonable to include 30 or 40 tasks on a 2-minute quiz. Yet this tends to be the exception, not the rule.

If extended response tasks are used (the topic of the next chapter), the teacher has to consider how long it will take for students to respond to each task. How long does it take students to perform a particular experiment? to write a comparative essay? to solve a multistage problem? As might be expected, only a few extended response tasks, perhaps as few as two or three, can be included in 100 minutes.

Regardless of the type of assessment task chosen by the teachers, these initial estimates need to be made. Eventually, these estimates should be revised after the assessment instruments have been administered to students.

Information on Each Objective

To make the decision for which the information is collected, is it necessary to have information about each assessed objective or is a more general set of information, across all assessed objectives, adequate or appropriate? The answer to this question determines in large part how the approximately 100 selection and/or short-response tasks will be divided among the objectives. For example, suppose the teacher decides to focus on eight objectives in a given unit. On average, there would be about 12 items for each objective (although the more complex objectives would likely have more, whereas the less complex objectives would have less). How reliable would our information be for each of these objectives? In chapter 1, we pointed out that a one-item test has little reliability. Quite clearly, a 12-item test would yield far more reliable information than a one-item test. In fact, the unit assessment can be considered a series of eight 12-item tests, one test per objective. With 12-items per objective, it is likely that the unit assessment would provide sufficiently reliable information to make decisions about individual student achievement on an objective-by-objective basis.

Suppose, however, that we decrease the assessment time by one half (from 100 minutes to 50) and we double the number of objectives (from 8 to 16). Now the situation is quite different. We would have, on average, about three items per objective. If decisions are to be made about individual students, three items per objective are less likely to provide reliable information on an objective-by-objective basis. However, if decisions about individual students can be based on information about general achievement of the unit objectives (e.g., assigning each student an overall grade on the unit), then the assessment will likely yield sufficiently reliable results. To make this decision, a total score for the entire unit assessment is computed for each student, rather than computing separate scores for each objective.

Although the information from this latter unit assessment may not be sufficiently reliable to make decisions about individual students on an objective-by-objective basis, it may be sufficiently reliable to make decisions about groups of students on individual objectives (e.g., for which objectives should I spend time reteaching?). As mentioned in chapter 1, the difference between decisions about individual students and groups of students is an important one. Typically, decisions about groups can be made on the basis of less reliable information than can decisions about individual students.

To reiterate, the first step in designing instruments to assess student achievement is to plan the curriculum on a unit-by-unit basis. Within each unit, teachers must decide which objectives are **worth assessing** and how many objectives **can be assessed reliably** given the amount of time spent on assessment and the decision(s) to be made based on the information obtained.

STEP 3: SELECT OR WRITE ASSESSMENT TASKS FOR EACH OBJECTIVE

Before selecting or writing assessment tasks, each assessable objective should be filtered through the Taxonomy Table (see chap. 2) to ensure that the teacher understands the meaning of each objective in terms of intended student learning. The placement of the objective in the proper cell(s) of the Taxonomy Table should be the basis for determining the **substance** of the assessment tasks. Does the objective call for students to remember factual knowledge, understand conceptual knowledge, or apply procedural knowledge? Does the objective call for students to analyze written material based on factual, conceptual, procedural, and, perhaps, metacognitive knowledge? Does the objective call for students to evaluate arguments, problem solutions, or the aesthetic value of artwork based on specified criteria (i.e., conceptual knowledge) and metacognitive knowledge? Does the objective call for students to create something based on metacognitive knowledge, as well as factual, conceptual, and/or procedural knowledge? Before teachers beginning searching for or writing assessment tasks, they must have a clear and precise understanding of what they are assessing. In working with several groups of teachers, I have found that the Taxonomy Table is a useful tool in this regard.

The Form of Assessment Tasks

In many life situations, we avoid substantive issues in favor of matters of form. What we look like becomes more important than who we are. So it is with classroom assessment. Multiple-choice, true–false, matching, and short-answer tasks are four forms, but they have no substance. The objective provides the substance for each of these forms.

It is important to note that these forms are more similar than they are different. In fact, they are best considered variations on a theme. This can be illustrated quite clearly if we consider the anatomy of an assessment task (see Fig. 3.1).

The heart of the assessment task is the **stem**. The stem can be a question to be answered, an incomplete statement to be completed, or a directive to be followed (e.g., "do this," "write this," "solve this"). In essence, the stem alone can be an assessment task. "What is the capital of Louisiana?" "The scientific name for an animal without a backbone is a(n) _____." "Simplify: $2x + 3(x - 5) + 15$." Note that in these examples the response required to complete each task is implicit in the stem. This is true whether

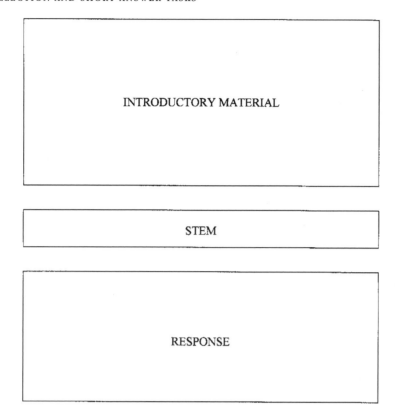

FIG. 3.1   The anatomy of an assessment task.

the stem is a question (Example 1), an incomplete sentence (Example 2), or a directive (Example 3).

In responding to any of these assessment tasks, students could be asked to supply an answer (as they are currently written) or select an answer (if response options were provided). So the **response** is the second piece of the anatomy puzzle. Short-answer tasks require students to supply an answer (and, obviously, a short one). In contrast, multiple-choice, true–false, and matching tasks require students to select the correct, best, or most defensible answer from among a set of alternatives.

For some assessment tasks, students need additional information to respond properly to the stem. If the student is expected to detect a problem in an electrical circuit, for example, a verbal description or pictorial representation of the circuit is needed. Similarly, if a student is expected to use context clues to determine the meaning of the word *ingenuous*, a sentence in which the word is used is needed. In some cases, the sentence may need to be embedded in a paragraph for the meaning of the word to be clear. These verbal descriptions, pictorial representations, paragraphs, and the like can be referred to as ***introductory material***. It should be clear that not all assessment tasks require introductory material. In fact, none of the three examples mentioned earlier does.

Having examined the anatomy of an assessment task, let us now return to the connections among the four forms of assessment tasks mentioned earlier: short answer, multiple-choice, true–false, and matching. All have stems, and all may or may not require introductory material. Short-answer tasks require that students supply a response, whereas the others require that students select a response from a given set of options. Among the multiple-choice, true–false, and matching formats, the multiple-choice format is the general case of which the other two can be derived. To illustrate this, consider the examples in Fig. 3.2 and 3.3. As shown in Fig. 3.2, true–false tasks and two-option multiple-choice tasks are virtually identical. Similarly, matching tasks are just repeated multiple-choice tasks (Fig. 3.3).

Rather than present grocery lists of dos and don'ts for writing assessment tasks of various formats, it seems more reasonable to focus on three basic principles. First, be clear. Second, be reasonable. Third, do not give the answer away. The first principle applies primarily to the **introductory material** and **stem**. It includes concerns for providing clear directions, using appropriate vocabulary, and avoiding ambiguous and confusing wording and sentence structure. The second principle applies primarily to the **responses**, particularly the response options included in multiple-choice and matching tasks. This principle includes concerns for plausible response options that are logically organized and belong to a single category of responses (i.e., homogeneity of responses). The third principle applies

---

Multiple-Choice Task
Is CO_2 the chemical formula for carbon monoxide?   a. Yes, it is.   b. No, it is not.

True-False Task
CO_2 is the chemical formula for carbon monoxide.   True   False

FIG. 3.2   The parallelism of multiple-choice and true–false tasks.

Multiple-Choice Tasks

---

1. The sentence, "Terrific Tom tames terrible tigers" is an example of:
   a. Alliteration
   b. Hyperbole
   c. Metaphor
   d. Personification

2. The sentence, "I caught a fish that weighed as much as the boat" is an example of:
   a. Alliteration
   b. Hyperbole
   c. Metaphor
   d. Personification

3. The sentence, "Peter is the workhorse of the company" is an example of:
   a. Alliteration
   b. Hyperbole
   c. Metaphor
   d. Personification

Matching Task

Match the literary device in Column B with the appropriate sentence in Column A.
Column A)

COLUMN A	COLUMN B
1. I caught a fish that weighed as much as the boat.	a. Alliteration
2. Peter is the workhorse of the company.	b. Hyperbole
3. Terrific Tom tames terrible tigers.	c. Metaphor
	d. Personification

FIG. 3.3   The parallelism of multiple-choice and matching tasks.

to the relationships between and among the **introductory material**, **stems**, and **responses**. It includes avoiding grammatical clues; avoiding the use of words such as *always, all, never,* and *none*; keeping response options the same length; and varying the position of the correct answer. Table 3.2 contains a list of frequently encountered item writing guidelines organized according to these three principles.

Linking Form With Substance

Simply stated, the craft of writing assessment tasks involves finding ways to link form with substance. The choice of the word *craft* in the prior sentence is important. In the past, teachers have practiced the art of writing assessments tasks, whereas assessment specialists have attempted to make

TABLE 3.2
Guidelines for Writing Selection-Type and Short-Answer Assessment Tasks

Criterion	Specific Guideline	Task Format
Be clear	Provide clear directions (including basis for determining answers, how to mark answers, whether response options in matching tasks can be used more than once).	All
	State the task or problem clearly and succinctly.	All
	Use questions whenever possible (MC, SA). If statements are used, word them positively (TF) and place the blank at the end of the statement (SA).	MC, SA
		TF
	Use appropriate vocabulary.	All
	Avoid ambiguous and confusing wording and sentence structure.	All
	Avoid including superfluous information.	All
	In matching tasks, write longer premises (entries in left-hand column) and shorter response options (entries in right-hand column should).	Matching
Be reasonable	Make sure all response options are homogeneous (i.e., members of some larger category).	MC, Matching
	Organize response options logically (e.g., alphabetical, chronological, numerical order).	MC, Matching
	Write options that are plausible and equally attractive to uninformed students.	MC, Matching
	Use a reasonable number of response options.Make sure that only only option/answer is correct or clearly best.	MC, Matching
	Specify the precision of the answer (including measurement units).	SA
	Avoid using all of the above and use none of the above with caution.	MC
	Use blanks that are long enough for handwritten answers.	SA
Do not give the answer away	Keep response options approximately the same length.	TF, MC
	Avoid specific determiners (e.g., always, all, never, none, every).	TF
	Avoid grammatical clues (e.g., a vs. an at end of incomplete sentence stem).	All
	Avoid repeating wording from the stem in the correct response option.	MC, Matching
	Vary the position of the correct answer.	MC
	In matching tasks, have more response options (right-hand column) than premises (left-hand column).	Matching

the writing of assessment tasks a science. Teachers would put together their quizzes by reflecting on what they thought was important to assess and then getting their thoughts on paper in some form or another. In contrast, assessment specialists spent a great deal of time attempting to establish rules and specifications for generating assessment tasks. An example of the result of these efforts is shown in Table 3.3.

A craft is a little bit art and a little bit science. The science provides the criteria and procedures, whereas the art provides the flexibility to operate within these criteria and procedures. The Taxonomy Table provides the structure of the tasks used to assess student achievement. In chapter 2, it was argued that a large number of objectives fall within three cells of the Taxonomy Table: Remember Factual Knowledge, Understand Conceptual Knowledge, and Apply Procedural Knowledge. For discussion purposes, let us focus on the cell Understand Conceptual Knowledge.

Referring back to Table 2.3, we can see that there are a number of ways to determine whether a student understands conceptual knowledge. Based on the entries in that table, a student understands conceptual knowledge if he or she can:

- Change from one form of presentation (e.g., numerical) to another (e.g., verbal);
- Find a specific example or illustration of a concept or principle;
- Determine that something new does or does not belong to a category;
- Abstract a general theme or major point;
- Draw a logical conclusion from presented information;
- Detect correspondences between two ideas, objects, and the like; and
- Construct a cause-and-effect model of a system.

In chapter 2, I suggested that the stem "Which of these is an example of X?" followed by four response options could be a prototype task for assessing students' understanding of conceptual knowledge. More specifically, this prototype would be linked with the third bullet. Similar prototypes can be developed for each of the remaining bullets. Armed with these prototypes, large numbers of assessment tasks aligned with key objectives can be written. The substance of these prototypes would be derived from the objectives; the choice of form (or format) would be made on the basis of the appropriate fit between substance and form.

Writing and Locating Assessment Tasks

Once prototypes are written (and they can be written for all of the cells of the Taxonomy Table, not just those most frequently encountered), the job becomes writing or locating specific assessment tasks that embody the pro-

TABLE 3.3
An Example of an Item Specification Chart

Descriptive Title	Sample Item	General Form	Generation Rules[a]
Basic fact; minuend > 10	13 $-\ 6$	A $-\ B$	1. $A = 1a; B = b$ 2. $(a < b) \in U$ 3. $\{H, V\}$
Simple borrow; one-digit subtrahend	53 $-\ 7$	A $-\ B$	1. $A = a_1 a_2 : B = b$ 2. $a_1 \in U - \{1\}$ 3. $(b > a_2) \in U_0$
Borrow across 0.	403 $-\ 138$	A $-\ B$	1. $N \in \{3, 4\}$ 2. $A = a_1 a_2 \ldots ; B = b_1 b_2 \ldots$ 3. $(a_1 > b_1), (a_3 < b_3),$ $\quad (a_1 \geq b_1) \in U_0$ 4. $b_2 \in U_0$ 5. $a_2 = 0$ 6. $P\ \{\{1, 2, 3\}, \{4\}\}$
Equation; missing subtrahend	$42 - \underline{\quad} = 25$	$A - \underline{\quad} = B$	1. $A = a_1 a_2 ; B = b_1 b_2$ 2. $a_1 \in U$ 3. $a_2 ; b_1 ; b_2 \in U_0$ 4. *Check:* $0 < B < A$

Explanation of notation:

   Capital letters A, B … represent numerals.

   Small letters (with or without subscripts), a, b, a_1, b_2, etc., represent digits.

   $x \in \{ \ldots \}$: Choose at random a replacement for x from the given set.

   a, b, c, $\in \{ \ldots \}$: All of a, b, c are chosen from the given set *with replacement*.

   N_A: Number of digits in numeral A.

   N: Number of digits in each numeral in the problem.

   a_1, a_2, … $\in \{ \ldots \}$: Generate all the a_1 necessary. In general " … " means continue the pattern established.

   $(a < b) \in \{ \ldots \}$: Choose two numbers at random *without* replacement; let a be the smaller.

   $\{H, V\}$: Choose a horizontal or vertical format.

   $P\ \{A, B, \ldots \}$: Choose a permutation of the elements in the set. (If the set consists of subscripts, permute those subscripted elements.)

   Set operations are used as normally defined. Note that $A - B = A \cap \overline{B}$. Ordered pairs are also used as usual.

   Check: If a check is not fulfilled, regenerate all elements involved in the *check* statement (and any elements dependent on them).

Special sets:

   $U = \{1, 2, \ldots, 9\}$

   $U_0 = \{0, 1, \ldots, 9\}$

   Source: Glaser and Nitko (1971).

totype. To write appropriate response options for the stem "Which of these is an example of iambic pentameter?," a teacher needs to understand (a) the concept of iambic pentameter; (b) other poetic meters such iambic tetrameter, trochaic pentameter; and (c) his or her students, the instruction they have received, and the misunderstandings they are likely to possess. Armed with this understanding, a teacher may decide to use these four response options:

- A line of iambic pentameter (the correct answer);
- A line of iambic tetrameter;
- A line of anapestic pentameter;
- A line of anapestic hexameter.

The prototypes, then, provide the framework for writing the assessment tasks related to this objective. Teachers add the knowledge needed to write the actual tasks within those frameworks. This teacher knowledge may also lead to a revision of the prototype. In the prior example, a teacher may decide that the way it is written results in lengthy response options and that a revision of the prototype is in order. In the revised prototype, a short poem would be used as **introductory material**. The **stem** would be as follows: "Which of the following meters is illustrated in the above poem?" The **response options** would then consist of iambic pentameter, iambic tetrameter, trochaic pentameter, and trochaic octameter.

In addition to providing frameworks, prototypes allow teachers (and others) to work together to produce assessment tasks. This, I believe, is critical to the development of high-quality assessment tasks. In fact, the next step of the procedure requires that others become involved in the design of instruments for the purpose of assessing student achievement.

Finally, prototypes enable teachers to search out assessment tasks that already exist and may be appropriate for their use. Many years ago, I attended a meeting at which the issue of developing item specifications (such as the one in Table 3.3) arose. The objective under consideration was that students should be able to identify or determine the main idea of a paragraph or longer passage. At one point in the discussion, I suggested (somewhat tongue in cheek) that every possible item dealing with finding main ideas had already been written and they were lying in countless drawers in teachers' desks throughout the country (and perhaps the world). If we could but locate all of these items, we would not have to spend our time developing item specifications.

What I was arguing for (and still argue for) is the development of item banks or item pools. In preparing this book, I went online to search for all of the item banks or item pools that I could find. The results of my search are displayed in Table 3.4. At first blush, it may seem that the idea of item

TABLE 3.4
Collections of Item Banks and Item Pools

Published Works

Educational Testing Service. (1991). Algebra tests: Annotated bibliography of tests. Princeton, NJ: Author. (ERIC Document Number: ED 369792)

Educational Testing Service. (1991). Chemistry, grades 7–12: Annotated bibliography of tests. Princeton, NJ: Author. (ERIC Document Number: ED 368740)

Educational Testing Service. (1990). Criterion-referenced measures, grades 4–6: Annotated bibliography of tests. Princeton, NJ: Author. (ERIC Document Number: ED 368744)

Educational Testing Service. (1990). Criterion-referenced measures, grade 7 and above: Annotated bibliography of tests. Princeton, NJ: Author. (ERIC Document Number: ED 368745)

Purushothaman, M. (1975). Secondary mathematics item bank. Slough: National Foundation for Educational Research (NFER).

Rentz, R. R., & Bashaw, W. L. (1977). The national reference scale for reading: An application of the Rasch model. Journal of Educational Measurement, 14, 161–179.

Woodcock, R. W. (1974). Woodcock Reading Mastery Test. Circle Pines, MN: American Guidance Services.

Web Sites

www.examgen.com. This site provides item banks for secondary mathematics, science, and social studies.

www.english-forum.com. This site contains a variety of materials, including item banks, for reading and language arts.

banks/pools is outdated. After all, there are no citations after 1991. I believe, however, there is (or is soon to be) a resurgence of item banks/pools. My belief is partly supported by the two Web sites included in Table 3.4, as well as a Web site that is not included—namely the Web site of the Utah Department of Education (UDOE). This Web site is not included because only "Utah teachers with current teaching assignments" have access to it. Furthermore, these teachers "are asked to not share this material with others." This is a shame because item banks and item pools have such great potential to link assessment with instruction, by linking the tasks that we provide students to facilitate their learning with those we administer to them to determine what and how well they have learned. In fact, there is some evidence that teachers who have access to item bank and item pools have students who receive higher scores on standardized achievement tests (see, e.g., Bartley, 1997).

Before moving to the next section, I must emphasize that my comments about the UDOE Web site are not meant as a criticism of the UDOE. Developing large numbers of high-quality assessment tasks at the state level is not an easy task. In response to one of the FAQs included on the Web site, the following statements are made: "The item pools are a work in progress.... It is taking approximately 7–10 days for each subject at a particular grade level."

Rather, my comments are directed toward educators in general. We need to work together and share our knowledge and efforts if we are to address the fundamental problem of educating all our children (Bloom, 1981). This problem is much larger than any single person, school, school district, or state.

STEP 4: REVIEW ASSESSMENT TASKS

This is typically a short step, but an important one. It was Robert Burns, the Scottish poet, who wrote:

> But, Mousie, thou art no thy lane
> In proving foresight may be vain:
> The best laid schemes o' mice an' men
> Gang aft agley,
> An' lea'e us nought but grief an' pain
> For promis'd joy.

In the vernacular, what we plan does not always come to fruition. When it does not, we are disappointed. We know what we want to say, but sometimes we just do not say it. We know what we want to accomplish, but we just do not get there. So it is with assessment tasks. After we write an assessment task, we need to have someone take a look at it before we include it on an assessment instrument.

Ideally, this someone would be a teacher with whom we are working on a regular basis—someone we trust; someone on our team. Yet this is not always possible. If it were, we could exchange assessment tasks. You show me yours, I'll show you mine.

Regardless of who is chosen, there are certain things to which you want them to attend. You just do not give them the assessment tasks and say, "Take a look at these, will you?" They should review the tasks for redundancies, ambiguities, and other structural difficulties. That is, you want them to review the form of the tasks, but you also want them to review their substance. You want to know whether the task is related to the intended objective. You want to know whether the task is appropriate for the students for whom it is intended. You want to know whether it is too difficult or too easy. Based on the reviewer's comments, you may need to make alterations. Over time, however, your initial drafts get better and better.

Finally, there may be situations in which an external reviewer is not available. In this case, I would agree with Airaisan's (1997) suggestion that a "teacher should wait one day and reread them [the items]. Proofreading will help identify flaws in the items that can be corrected before test administration" (p. 179).

STEP 5: PREPARE UNIT ASSESSMENT(S)

Now comes the time that the assessment tasks are assembled into one or more instruments. This is not a trivial matter. Directions need to be written, and the tasks need to be arranged in some logical manner. Gronlund (2002) recommended that directions include the following:

- Purpose (i.e., why students are being assessed and how the results are used);
- Time allowed for completing the assessment;
- Basis for responding (e.g., Are they to choose the correct or best answer?);
- Procedures for recording answers (e.g., circle, darken the space, write answer); and, if applicable,
- What to do about guessing (i.e., Is there a penalty for guessing? Should students attempt to respond to each assessment task?).

Once directions have been written, attention next turns to the arrangement of the assessment tasks on the instrument. An efficient arrangement should make scoring easy for the teacher and should not present any obstacles to the students. One way to accomplish this is to arrange the tasks by their format and, within that format, from easy to difficult. The preferred arrangement—selection, then short answer, then essay—is illustrated in Fig. 3.4.

Grouping items of a similar format together is efficient in two ways. First, it allows you to write directions for each group of tasks. This saves time for both the teacher and his or her students. Second, by putting the directions above the first item of each format, it signals to the students that a change in format is coming. Thus, they do not have to shift back and forth between formats as they complete the assessment instrument. In addition to these major issues, there are several considerations that, if followed, lead to a more attractive and professional assessment instrument. These considerations are shown in Table 3.5. When considered as a set, the point is quite clear: Assessment instruments should be as error free and professionally looking as possible.

Your Name _____   Date _____

Directions. The purpose of this test is to determine how much you learned about polynomials during the past three weeks. You will receive a grade on this test, and I also will use the results to determine whether we need to review any of the material we covered. You will have exactly one hour to complete the test. The test is divided into three sections: multiple-choice, short-answer, and essay. Directions for each of these sections are given just prior to the section.

Multiple-Choice (directions)

1. Easiest item.
2.
3.
4.
5.
6.
7.
8.
9. Most difficult item.

Short-Answer (directions)

10. Easiest item.
11.
12.
13.
14.
15.
16.
17.
18. Most difficult item.

Essay Items (directions)

19.
20.

FIG. 3.4   Arrangement of tasks on a paper-and-pencil assessment instrument.

STEP 6: PREPARE METHOD OF SCORING STUDENT RESPONSES

For instruments containing solely selection and short-answer tasks, this is an easy step. You have to prepare a scoring key—that is, a list of right or best answers. For four-option multiple-choice tests, for example, the scor-

TABLE 3.5
Issues in the Preparation of Paper-and-Pencil Assessment Instruments

1.	Number tasks consecutively and leave an appropriate amount of space between tasks (so they do not look so crowded).
2.	Leave appropriate space for students to respond and arrange response options to make it as easy for students to respond as possible.
3.	If a task requires introductory material, place the introductory material on the same page as the stem and response options or prompt.
4.	Make the assessment instrument look as official and professional as possible. Typing or word processing is preferable to hand writing.
5.	Proofread the final copy of the assessment instrument carefully. Correct any typos, mistakes, or errors.

ing key would consist of a series of letters "a" through "d" (e.g., 1a, 2c, 3c, 4a, 5d, 6c, 7b, etc.). For short-answer tasks, the scoring key would consist of the correct short answers. For short-answer tasks, teachers would be wise to consider possible variations in advance. If the correct answer is "24 ounces," will "24" count? If the correct answer is "Andrew Jackson," will "Jackson" count? If these variations can be anticipated, then the directions given to students can ensure they know what is expected of them. "Your answers will need to include the unit of measurement." "Your answers will need to include the full name of people." If your directions are this precise, you will have less difficulty justifying "Jackson" or "24" as being incorrect.

STEP 7: ADMINISTER THE ASSESSMENT(S)

When administering student achievement assessment instruments, teachers should be aware of both the physical and psychological environments. The physical environment should be quiet and comfortable, with every attempt made to exclude outside disruptions. In establishing a proper psychological environment, teachers must walk the fine line between "this is the most important test of your life" and "this test doesn't matter at all." Teachers should tell students they should do their best on all their work and this test is no different. Also teachers should emphasize that each student is to do his or her own work, that cheating will not be tolerated, and that anyone caught cheating will be dealt with at the end of the testing session. Also to minimize cheating, students should be seated so that copying from another student is extremely difficult.

During the administration, teachers should monitor the assessment and keep track of time. In many respects, physical proximity of teachers to students is the primary deterrent of cheating. If any student is suspected of cheating, observed details should be noted in writing as soon as possible. Finally, it is useful if the teacher occasionally reminds students of the time remaining (e.g., "You will have 10 minutes to complete the test"). Reminders about half-way through the assessment period, then at 10 minutes, 5 minutes, and 2 minutes remaining, seem reasonable.

The administration of statewide assessments or nationally-normed tests provides additional challenges for teachers. The most important part of administering these tests is following the directions carefully and explicitly (McMillan, 1997). Teachers should familiarize themselves with the directions before they read them to their students. Directions should be read word for word, not paraphrased. Finally, once the testing session is over, teachers must account for all copies of the test and all answer sheets to ensure test security.

STEP 8: ANALYZE RESULTS OF THE ASSESSMENT(S)

The first time an assessment instrument is administered to a group of students, more is learned about the instrument than about the students. This is why commercial test publishers field test their instruments before releasing them to the public. What do you learn about the instrument? In a nutshell, you learn how the instrument actually functions in the field. Are the tasks that you thought would be difficult for students truly difficult for them? Are the responses to all of the items sufficiently consistent to justify a total score? Are the response options truly viable alternatives to the correct or best option? Are the incorrect answers that students give to short-answer tasks those that you would expect them to give? Notice that each of the questions presupposes that you bring some expectations to the table. This step, then, involves comparing your expectations with harsh reality.

Examining Individual Tasks

A good place to start is to look at the responses students actually make to each task. Begin by calculating the percentage of students who responded correctly or, in the vernacular, who got the item right. Because you are assessing students following some period of instruction and because you are assessing only those objectives you believe to be most important, tasks that fewer than half the students answered correctly should be viewed with suspicion. For each of these tasks, examine the responses given by those who missed the task to see whether they provide any clues. Airasian (1997) told the story of a social studies teacher who taught a unit on the "low countries" of Europe. On the unit assessment, she included the following question: "What are the low countries?" She expected "Belgium, Luxembourg, and the

Netherlands." However, a fairly substantial number of students wrote: "A group of countries in Europe that are largely below sea level." A slight modification would fix this problem: "What are the names of the low countries?"

Similar problems exist when an incorrect response option on a multiple-choice or matching task is chosen by students more frequently that the correct one. What is it about that particular response option that attracts students? Again, we turn to Airasian (1997) for an example. A health teacher, having completed a unit on diet and exercise, included the following task on the unit assessment.

The main value of a daily exercise program is to:

a. eat less.
b. develop musculature.
c. raise intelligence.
d. keep physically fit.

The keyed answer was "b." Suppose, however, that more students chose "d" than "b." Furthermore, suppose no students chose "c." These results would suggest that a modification in this task is needed (either in the response options or in the wording of the stem).

We began this discussion by targeting those tasks that 50% or fewer of the students answered correctly. What about those tasks that 95% to 100% of the students get right? These are worth examining particularly in terms of principle number three of task preparation, "Don't give the answer away." Does the task include specific determiners, grammatical clues, or repetitious words in the stem and correct answer? If it does, revise accordingly. If it does not, you may have a victory for good teaching.

A fairly simple table can be used to facilitate the examination of individual tasks (see Table 3.6). The rows of the table correspond with the students who were assessed; the columns of the table correspond with the assessment tasks. Rather than appearing in numerical order, however, the tasks are organized around the objectives they are intended to assess. In addition, students are placed in the table according to their overall score on the assessment instrument from highest to lowest.

To simplify the table, let us assume that the entire assessment instrument is composed of multiple-choice tasks. A "1" in a cell means that the student gave the correct answer. A letter in the cell indicates that (a) the answer was incorrect and (b) this was the choice ("a," "b," "c," "d") given by the student.

For teachers interested in improving their assessment instruments, Table 3.6 provides a wealth of information about individual assessment tasks. First, Tasks 1, and 12 were answered correct by 18 (100%) of the students. Are these legitimate tasks or are clues to the correct response embedded

TABLE 3.6

Summary of the Results for 18 Students Completing a 20-Item Test

Student Task Number	Objective 1				Objective 2				Objective 3						Objective 4			Objective 5			RT
	1	5	8	13	2	10	14	15	3	7	11	16	17	18	4	9	19	6	12	20	
Vernon	1	1	1	1	1	1	1	1	1	1	1	1	1	1	1	1	1	1	1	1	20
Felicia	1	1	1	1	1	1	1	1	1	1	1	1	1	1	1	1	1	1	1	1	20
Wells	1	1	1	1	1	1	1	1	1	d	1	1	1	1	1	1	1	1	1	1	19
Kitty	1	b	1	1	1	1	1	1	1	d	1	1	1	1	1	b	c	1	1	1	17
David	1	b	1	1	1	1	1	1	1	d	1	1	1	1	a	1	1	1	1	1	17
Jordan	1	c	1	c	1	1	1	1	1	d	1	1	1	1	1	1	a	1	1	1	16
Michael	1	d	1	1	1	1	1	1	1	a	1	1	1	1	1	b	c	1	1	1	16
Jackson	1	1	1	1	1	1	1	1	1	a	1	1	1	1	1	b	a	d	1	1	15
Janice	1	c	1	1	1	1	1	1	c	a	1	1	1	1	1	b	a	d	1	1	15
Alice	1	c	1	1	1	1	1	1	1	d	1	1	1	b	c	c	1	d	1	1	14
Betty	1	1	1	1	1	1	1	b	d	a	1	1	1	1	d	b	1	d	1	b	14
Steve	1	1	1	c	1	a	1	a	1	d	1	1	a	1	a	1	1	d	1	c	13
Merrill	1	d	1	d	1	1	a	d	1	a	1	1	a	1	c	1	a	1	1	a	13
Connie	1	1	1	d	1	1	1	1	c	d	1	1	1	1	d	b	c	d	1	1	12
Jody	1	1	1	c	1	1	a	1	c	d	1	1	b	1	c	d	c	1	1	1	12
Becky	1	1	a	c	1	c	a	1	c	a	1	d	b	b	a	1	c	1	1	1	11
Russ	1	1	1	1	b	1	1	1	c	d	c	1	1	b	d	b	c	1	1	a	10
Mike	1	b	1	c	b	d	a	1	1	d	1	a	d	1	c	b	c	1	1	1	9
CT	18	11	17	12	17	15	14	15	13	2	17	16	13	15	8	9	7	12	18	14	

within them? Second, Tasks 4, 7, and 19 were answered correctly by fewer than half the students. Why are these tasks so difficult? Third, students who responded incorrectly to Tasks 6 and 14 (and to a slightly lesser extent Task 3) gave the same incorrect response. Does this suggest that they are all learning the same thing even though it is wrong? Fourth, no one chose option "b" for Task 3, option "c" for Task 7, or option "a" for Task 13. Are these plausible distractors? These are the types of questions that teachers can and should ask the first time they administer a student achievement assessment instrument.

Because students are placed in the table in order of their total scores on the assessment instrument, there is yet another way of looking at the data in Table 3.6. This requires us to look at each task within the context of the entire assessment instrument (and provides a link to the next section). The logic behind this examination is as follows. Those students who do the best on the entire set of tasks should do better on each assessment task than those who do more poorly on the entire set of tasks. In traditional measurement terms, this is known as item discrimination (Airasian, 1997; Gallagher, 1998). In terms of the entries in Table 3.6, this means that you should see more "1s" near the top of the table in each column and more letters (a, b, c, and d) near the bottom. In Table 3.6, this is true for all tasks except Tasks 1, 6, 12, and 15. With respect to Tasks 1 and 12, it is important to note that all students responded correctly. Hence, no differentiation among students is possible. Task 15 is interesting in that the top five scoring students and the bottom five scoring students gave the correct response. It was the students in the middle of the achievement distribution who tended to respond incorrectly to the task. A similar pattern emerges for Task 6.

Examining Sets of Tasks

As suggested in Table 3.6, instruments designed to assess student achievement have an **implicit organization** that is different from the **explicit organization** of the instrument. In the vernacular, what you see is not exactly what you get. The explicit organization was discussed in Step 7. The explicit organization is what you see and is a matter of form (or format). However, the implicit organization conforms to the way in which tasks, objectives, and the instrument are interrelated (see Fig. 3.5).

This organization can be described using terminology shared by educational researchers (and, perhaps, ornithologists). Simply stated, assessment tasks are nested within objectives that, in turn, are nested within assessment instruments. This nested structure permits us to examine sets (or collections) of tasks. Specifically, we can examine the tasks related to each objective. We can also examine the entire set of tasks included on the assessment instrument. The focus of this examination is the consistency of

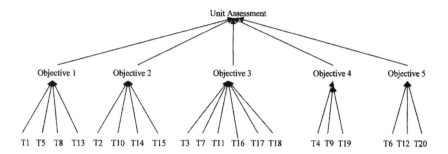

FIG. 3.5   Structure of unit assessment instruments.
Note: T1, T2, T3, ... T20 indicate the 20 tasks included on the assessment instrument. Notice that the tasks associated with each objective are not in sequential order. As discussed earlier, the arrangement of the tasks on assessment instruments depends on the task format, not the objective.

responses made by students to these sets of tasks. Using traditional measurement terminology, we are examining the reliability of the data.

Looking at Table 3.6 from this perspective, several other interesting issues arise. With respect to Objective 2, for example, students did equally well on all four tasks, with between 16 and 19 students giving correct responses. In contrast, students did relatively poorly on all three tasks associated with Objective 4. Students did very well on two of the tasks related to Objective 1, but rather poorly on the other two. What accounts for this difference in student performance? With respect to Objective 3, students performed reasonably well on five of the six tasks, the exception being Task 7. Interestingly, we already had some concern about Task 7 based on our task-by-task analysis. Similarly, Task 12 seems somewhat easier than the other two tasks associated with Objective 5. Once again, however, we identified Task 12 as worthy of further examination during our task-by-task analysis.

There is one final way to empirically examine the relationships among the tasks, objectives, and assessment instrument. This is to estimate what is referred to as *internal consistency reliability*. There are six estimates of internal consistency reliability inherent in Fig. 3.5. Estimates can be made for each of the five objectives as well as for the overall assessment instrument.

There are many ways to estimate internal consistency. The most common are estimates based on the split-half method, the Kuder–Richardson formulas, and the computation of Cronbach's alpha (see e.g., Gallagher, 1998). For teachers without computers, the split-half method is clearly the easiest. The number of estimates that need to be made depends on the nature of the decision that needs to be made. If decisions are to be made on an objective-by-objective basis, then five estimates—one for each objective—are needed. However, if decisions are to be made based on the overall performance of students on the assessment instrument, then only one estimate is needed.

Regardless of the number of estimates needed, the split-half method of estimating internal consistency reliability is quite straightforward. As the name suggests, the first step is to split the tasks into two sets. One reasonable way to do this is to separate even-numbered from odd-numbered tasks, taking into consideration differences in the objectives with which the tasks are aligned. Next, calculate each student's scores for the odd- and even-numbered tasks. If the two scores are identical or similar, the scores are internally consistent—hence, reliable. If there are wide disparities between the scores on the odd- and even-numbered tasks, then we have a problem. Such would likely be the case for Objective 1 in Table 3.6. Obviously, this method only works when there is an even number of tasks per objective. When there are an odd number of tasks, modifications must be made or alternative methods must be used. In addition to objective-by-objective estimates, this same method can be used to estimate the internal consistency reliability of the entire assessment instrument. For the more computer-oriented teacher, internal consistency reliability estimates are built into most test analysis or statistical analysis computer software packages. Table 3.6 is already in the format used by these packages.

STEP 9: ASSIGNING STUDENT SCORES

When using selection and short-answer tasks, the computation of student scores is quite straightforward. You simply add up the number of tasks to which the student has responded correctly. In Table 3.6, these are the row totals (RTs). The "fly in the ointment" is how to handle the *problematic* tasks that were identified in Step 8. One approach, clearly the most common, is to ignore them and let the scores initially assigned to students stand. A second approach is to eliminate the problematic items and recalculate the scores for each student. Decisions would then be made on the basis of these recalculated scores. If this option is chosen, I suggest that the **percentage** of tasks responded to correctly should be used instead of the **number** of tasks. Percentages are less likely to change when tasks are eliminated. For example, 16 correct out of 20 tasks is not sufficiently different from 13 correct out of 16 (supposing that 4 items are eliminated). Furthermore, decreases in numbers are likely to be interpreted as lowering the standards in making decisions. Continuing with the previous example, 13 correct is notably fewer than 16 correct.

STEP 10: SAVE ASSESSMENT INSTRUMENTS
AND ASSESSMENT RESULTS

Kehoe (1995) summarized the general objectives of someone who intends to design high-quality assessment instruments in the following way:

> As a rule, one is concerned with writing stems that are clear and parsimonious, answers that are unequivocal and chosen by the students who do best on the test, and distractors that are plausible competitors of the answer as evidenced by the frequency with which they are chosen. Lastly, and probably most important, we should adopt the attitude that [assessment tasks] need to be developed over time in light of [empirical evidence] and ... "expert" editorial review. (p. 1)

The first part of this quotation summarizes many of the points already made in this chapter. The second part is the subject of this short closing section. Designing good assessment instruments is hard work; it involves trial, error, and revision. Consequently, it makes little sense to administer an instrument and then throw it away along with the data obtained from its administration.

This final step of the process outlined in this chapter reminds teachers to save and build on their work. Rather than disposing of it and starting from scratch each term or year, place the instrument, the summary of students' responses to the instrument (as in Table 3.6), and notes you have made about how the instrument can be improved in a file folder. In this way, the materials in the folder can be used as the basis for developing a more technically sound assessment instrument the next time the unit is taught. Obviously, alterations need to be made as the content and structure of the unit are changed. At the same time, however, building on one's previous work is preferable to rediscovering the wheel over and over. This latter approach virtually guarantees that no progress is made.

CHAPTER FOUR

Assessing Student Achievement Using Extended Response and Performance Tasks

The focus of this chapter is alternative assessments (Herman, 1997). Alternative assessments differ from more conventional assessments primarily in terms of the responses that students are required to make. In alternative assessments, students are required or expected to **generate** an extended response to a task, rather than **select** a response or **supply** a short response (e.g., one, two, or perhaps three words). Quite clearly, however, different response expectations influence the structure of the entire assessment task. For example, the stem of the task must be one that encourages rather than restricts extended responses. The stem "Is it possible to divide a whole number by zero?" requires a simple "yes" or "no" answer. In contrast, the stem "Prove that it is impossible to divide a whole number by zero" calls for an extended response.

Although in most cases students are required to write these responses, there are alternative assessment tasks that require students to make or do something. Technically speaking, only these latter tasks should be referred to as *performance tasks*. In practice, however, the phrase *performance task* is used to denote any task that requires students to generate an extended response regardless of the nature of that response, written or otherwise. To avoid redundancy and, hopefully, minimize confusion, the phrase *extended response tasks* is used throughout this chapter because I believe it to be the more general term.

Authentic assessment is another phrase you might encounter when reading about alternative assessments. What makes assessment authentic? Once again, the answer resides in the nature and structure of the assessment tasks. Authentic assessment tasks are those with some connection to real-life situations, practical problems, or both (i.e., practical problems in real-life situations). To determine whether an assessment task is authentic, you simply have to ask yourself, "How likely is it that students will encounter a task like this outside of the classroom?" The more likely it is, the more authentic the task.

Is it appropriate to include authentic tasks on assessments of student achievement? Some would respond to this question with a resounding, "Yes, absolutely!" I take a bit more cautious approach. The answer to this question depends on whether the objectives set forth by the teacher call for students to engage in authentic learning. I question the wisdom of using authentic assessment tasks to assess the learning of students exposed to a steady diet of nonauthentic learning experiences and tasks. Furthermore, I am not a great supporter of using changes in assessments to stimulate changes in the curriculum, however popular this practice might be (i.e., "We **ex**pect what we **in**spect"). Rather, I think educators should have the courage to confront the value issue head on. What **is** important for students to learn? Then we should assess student achievement of what was/is deemed to be important. Stated simply, it is not assessment that is or is not authentic. It is the learning that is authentic to a greater or lesser degree. Consequently, the phrase *authentic assessment* should be replaced by *assessment of authentic learning*.

Authentic assessment tasks are related to extended response tasks, but not as clearly as many people think. Authentic assessment tasks typically require some type of extended response on the part of the student. However, the opposite is not true. That is, not all extended response tasks are authentic. Consider the prior examples concerning dividing by zero. Although the second task clearly requires an extended response, it is quite unlikely that students (other than future mathematicians) will encounter this situation in real life. Because the phrase *authentic assessment* applies more directly to the objectives than the assessment per se, it is not used beyond this point in the discussion.

Having clarified the meaning of various terms associated with alternative assessments and indicated that the phrase *extended response tasks* is used throughout, we can now move to issues involved in the design and development of alternative assessment instruments. The 10-step procedure described in the previous chapter applies to alternative assessments as well, with a few major adjustments needing to be made. Only those steps where clear differences between conventional assessments and alternative assessments are discussed in this chapter. Thus, Step 4 (review of the assessment tasks), Step 5 (preparation of the assessment instrument), Step 7 (administration of the assessment instrument), and Step 10 (maintenance of an assessment file folder) are not discussed. The same points made about these steps in chapter 3 apply here.

WHICH OBJECTIVES?

In Step 1, you were advised, within each curriculum unit, to determine which objectives were sufficiently important to assess. At that time, the point was made that large numbers of objectives typically fall into three cells of the Taxonomy Table: remembering factual knowledge, understanding conceptual knowledge, and applying procedural knowledge. As pointed out in chapter 3, selection and short-answer tasks can be used for all three of these categories of objectives. However, it would be absolutely ludicrous to use extended response tasks to assess remembering factual knowledge. The greatest value of extended response tasks lies in the assessment of understanding conceptual knowledge and so-called *higher order cognitive processes* (i.e., analyze, evaluate, and, especially, create).

Assessing Understanding of Conceptual Knowledge

Selection and short-answer tasks often focus on one concept or principle at a time (e.g., atomic mass, principle of the conversation of matter). Connections between and among sets of concepts are more difficult to assess using these types of tasks.

Furthermore, when we administer selection and short-answer tasks, we often learn more about what students **do not** understand than what they **do** understand. Even when a student responds correctly to a task, we are not always certain that he or she understands what is being assessed. In addition, unless a task is carefully crafted and examined response by response, we gain little information about what the students who give incorrect responses to the tasks actually **do** understand. Extended response tasks have great potential in these areas.

One approach, advocated by the National Center for Research on Evaluation, Standards, and Student Testing (CRESST), is the use of concept maps as an assessment tool. Concept maps may be classified as nonauthentic, extended response tasks. An example of a simple concept map is shown in Fig. 4.1.

Figure 4.1 contains four concepts: cat, dog, affection, and poodle. The top part of the figure simply presents these concepts as independent ovals. The directive given to students is to use arrows and words to describe the relationships among the concepts. The bottom part of the figure provides an example of one student's response to the directive. Cats scratch dogs; in reciprocation, dogs bite cats. Both cats and dogs give affection to people. A poodle is a kind of dog. This structured drawing represents the conceptual understanding of this student quite well. How many selection or short-answer tasks would you have to assign to equal this level of understanding?

A more complex concept map, one formatted for assessment purposes, is shown in Fig. 4.2. The directions appear at the top, the terms denoting the key concepts are located in the box at the left, and the ovals are placed

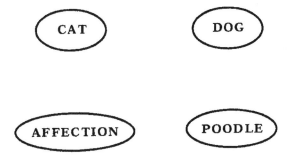

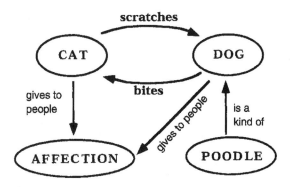

FIG. 4.1   Simple concept map.
CRESST. Reprinted with permission.

in various positions. Students are asked to write the terms in the ovals, use arrows to connect the ovals with other ovals, and write a few words near each arrow to "tell how the terms are related in your thinking."

Unstructured drawings and graphical representations also have potential in the assessment of conceptual understanding. For example, suppose a teacher has prepared a unit on volcanoes and earthquakes. Prior to teaching the unit, the teacher gives each student a poster-size sheet of paper and tells the students to draw a picture that explains how volcanoes erupt. They are to label the drawing and then write a brief paragraph describing it. Three weeks later, following instruction, students are asked to repeat the task. A comparison of the two pictures, sets of labels, and written de-

Directions: Now, draw a concept map using the 10 terms in the box below. They are related to photosynthesis. Write the terms in the bubbles below. Then draw lines with arrowheads on them between the bubbles to show which terms are related to each other. Then write one or a few words on each line to tell how the terms are related in your thinking. Remember, there isn't one "right answer." Everybody's map will be different. Just show the way YOU think about these things. Draw all the relationships you can think of that seem important.

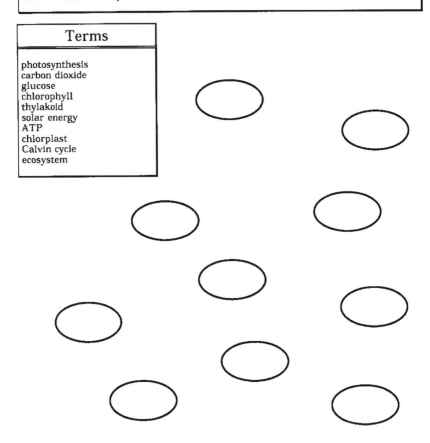

Terms

photosynthesis
carbon dioxide
glucose
chlorophyll
thylakoid
solar energy
ATP
chlorplast
Calvin cycle
ecosystem

FIG. 4.2   A more complex concept map.
CRESST. Reprinted with permission.

scriptions permits the teacher (as well as the students) to assess how much students' conceptual understanding has changed during the unit.

Concept maps and unstructured drawings enable teachers to gain a deeper understanding of their students' understanding. Referring back to Table 2.4, these assessment tasks focus on knowledge of theories, models, and structures (Bc). Theories, models, and structures provide the basis for the most sophisticated level of understanding that is possible.

One potential problem with concept maps concerns how they are scored. If a particular conceptual structure is expected as a result of instruction, then a template of that conceptual structure can be made (i.e., as a transparency). The template can be placed over the conceptual structure developed by each student and discrepancies noted (e.g., connections that were expected but are not there, connections that were not expected but are there). The number of discrepancies can be used as the total score.

Alternatively, as in the volcanoes and earthquakes example, the teacher would examine the pictures holistically. The focus would be on (a) an increase in understanding of the phenomenon of earthquake eruption over the course of the unit, and (b) an end-of-unit understanding of the phenomenon of earthquake eruption that is consistent with the shared scientific understanding. In this situation, some holistic scoring rubric would be developed and used to score the drawings. Scoring rubrics are discussed in great detail later in this chapter.

Assessing Problem Solving

Since the publication of Bloom's taxonomy in 1956, cognitive processes associated with analyze, evaluate, and create have traditionally been referred to as *higher order* or *higher level cognitive processes*. These processes include differentiating, organizing, attributing, checking, critiquing, generating, planning, and producing (see Table 2.3). These higher order cognitive processes are particularly important in the area of problem solving. To solve a problem, students have to *differentiate* relevant from irrelevant information. They have to *organize* the relevant information and *plan* a viable solution strategy. They have to *implement* the strategy and *monitor* their progress toward solving the problem, making adjustments as necessary.

Unfortunately, many educators view problem solving entirely from a cognitive process perspective. That is, they focus exclusively on the *italicized* verbs in the previous description. It is important to recognize that in problem solving, cognitive processes and knowledge work hand in hand. It is primarily factual knowledge that is separated into relevant and irrelevant information. It is primarily conceptual knowledge that provides the organization of the information. It is primarily procedural knowledge that is involved in attempting to solve the problem. Finally, it is primarily metacognitive knowledge that enables students to monitor their progress toward problem solution and make adjustments along the way.

Because of the complexity of problem solving and the interplay between and among cognitive processes and knowledge, assessment of both problem solving and higher order cognitive processes is difficult using se-

lection or short-answer tasks. For this type of achievement, there is a particular need to explore alternative assessments. Fortunately, a great deal of
progress has been made in this area thanks to the efforts of Grant Wiggins
(www.relearning.org), Rich Stiggins (www.assessmentinst.com), and the
entire staff of CRESST (www.cse.ucla.edu/CRESST). Examples of extended
response tasks for assessing problem solving are shown in Table 4.1.

Assessing the Process of Creating

Creating involves putting elements together to form a coherent or functional whole. It is important to emphasize that creating is not the same as
creativity. To some people, creativity is the design of unusual products or
generation of unique ideas often as a result of some special talent inherent
in the individual. Not everyone can be creative, in this sense of the word,
but everyone can create. Thus, objectives associated with the cognitive
process category, Create, call for students to produce their own synthesis
of information or materials to form a new whole, as in writing, painting,
sculpting, building, and so on. This synthesis is often required when the
student is expected to assemble previously taught material into an organized presentation, written or oral. Table 4.2 contains illustrations of objectives that require students to create something.

Objectives that require students to create something differ from those that
require them to engage in problem solving in one important respect. Creating
is a divergent activity. In the words of the immortal Forrest Gump, "You never
know what you're going to get." In contrast, problem solving is a convergent
activity. The problem is solved or it is not. This distinction is important because writing, speaking, and researching are not exclusively creative processes. Writing, speaking, and researching are part of problem solving as well.

Quite clearly, the objectives shown in Table 4.2 cannot be assessed
properly using selection and short-answer tasks. They must be assessed
with extended response tasks. Not surprisingly, then, numerous guidelines for assessing these objectives have been developed (as we see later
in this chapter).

THE TIME FRAME FOR COMPLETING
EXTENDED RESPONSE TASKS

Whereas students can respond to about one selection or short-answer type
task per minute, the time frame for completing extended response tasks is
much longer. It is rare to see an extended response task that requires fewer
than 10 or 20 minutes to complete. At this rate, teachers could assign only
two, three, or four such tasks per class period (more if a secondary school is
operating on a block schedule).

TABLE 4.1
Examples of Problem-Solving Tasks

Investigate the changes in the price of various technologies over time (e.g., radios, TVS, computers, CD players). Draw graphs to summarize your findings. Select a recently introduced technology and, based on your findings, estimate the price of new versions of this technology in 2010.

A pickup has run into the back of a car. Model the actual crash with a small dart gun and a model car and find alternative methods of determining the speed of the dart shot from the gun. Use your knowledge of conservation of momentum principles to determine the impact speed of the car.

A leading consumer magazine has hired you to answer the question, "Which antacid works best?" Using your knowledge of acid and base reactions, design and carry out an experiment to answer this question. Then prepare a report to the magazine detailing your results.

Locate a fairly large number of newspaper clippings about the World Trade Center disaster. Organize and read the clippings in chronological order. What turned out to be true? What turned out not to be true? What do we know at the present time? What remains to be known? Write a cohesive essay in which you address these four questions.

Wildlife officials and politicians are at odds because of the rare red-cockade woodpecker on the Fort Bragg military base. Fort Bragg officials have to limit military training exercises because of the protection required for the birds under the Endangered Species Act. Almost half the known red-cockade woodpecker population is located on the base. Propose a workable solution to the problem based on a careful review of the military's needs and the relevant law. Write a report and make a speech to a simulated EPA review board.

During the Iran-Contra trial, Oliver North testified that he bought a used van for $8,038 with the money he had saved by "taking change out of my pocket" every Friday for 20 years. He kept this change in a metal box bolted to the floor of his bedroom closet. He testified that he had accumulated over $15,000 during those 20 years. If you were a member of the jury, would you consider this reasonable? Write a paragraph to the judge explaining whether you consider Mr. North's testimony to be reasonable.

TABLE 4.2
Sample Objectives Requiring Students to Create

The student will learn to tell stories.

The student will learn to participate in historical role plays.

The student will learn to design and implement a public awareness campaign.

The student will learn to conduct interviews.

The student will learn to invent machines that accomplish simple tasks in a complex mechanical way (so-called Rube Goldberg machines).

The student will learn to conduct and report the results of sound, defensible research studies.

The student will learn to write for a variety of purposes.

The student will learn to formulate logical arguments about important issues.

Occasionally, as in the case of the examples shown in Tables 4.1 and 4.2, the assessment may take several days to complete, perhaps as long as a week. This increased time requirement raises two concerns about the use of extended response assessment tasks, both of which were mentioned earlier. The first concerns the relative proportion of time that should be spent on assessment vis à vis instruction (see chap. 3). Is it feasible to devote 1 week of a 4-week unit (25% of the allocated time) to assessment? This is a difficult question to answer under any circumstance, but particularly when teachers feel external pressure to cover particular content or a specific number of state-imposed standards. The second issue concerns the often blurred distinction between learning tasks and assessment tasks (see chap. 1). One way to save time for instruction within the context of alternative assessment is to use a task for both learning and assessment purposes. One can imagine, for example, a goodly portion of teaching going on as students work on the "changing price of technology" or "which antacid is best?" tasks in Table 4.1. This conflation of learning and assessment is not necessarily a bad thing, but could make defensible decision making difficult in certain situations (e.g., if student performance on the task is used to assign a unit grade, then who and what are being graded?).

WRITING EXTENDED RESPONSE ASSESSMENT TASKS

As can be seen by examining the sample tasks in Table 4.1, extended response tasks must be carefully crafted. Unlike many selection and short-answer tasks, extended response tasks generally include introductory material. The purpose of this introductory material is twofold: (a) to provide a context for the task (e.g., presidential request, fulfill job responsibilities), and (b) to provide task-specific directions (e.g., using your knowledge of conversation of momentum principles, select a recently introduced technology). Furthermore, the stem is often embedded within this introductory material, generally at the end (as in most of the examples in Table 4.1) or occasionally throughout (as in the "changing cost of new technologies" example).

Several experts in the field suggest that students should be made aware of the criteria used to evaluate the quality of the completed task, whether it is a finished product or an actual performance (see e.g., Baron, 1991; Stiggins, 2001). Although I concur with this recommendation, I do not believe this awareness should clutter up the task description. Rather, the evaluation guidelines should be given to students at the same time that they receive the task.

Why is it important for students to be aware of the evaluation criteria? Because with most extended response assessment tasks the objectives are inherent in the evaluation criteria, not in the description of the task. Consider the extended response task shown in Table 4.3. In essence, students are asked to design a switch for someone who does not have the use of his or her hands. What objectives are being assessed with this task? We could make a guess: Students were expected to learn how to apply knowledge of electrical circuits to real-life problems. Yet a more precise and defensible answer to this question is possible if you consider the evaluation criteria.

There are four evaluation criteria. The first "looks at whether or not students can at least draw a circuit with a battery and a light bulb." As an explanation for the inclusion of this criterion, the authors of the task wrote that the students "first need a basic understanding of what a simple circuit is and how to construct one." So the first implicit objective is that students will understand a simple circuit and how to construct one. The second criterion "looks simply for a circuit and switch that would effectively work to power and control a light." This criterion is related to a second objective: Students will understand how a switch works to power and control a light. The third criterion is whether the switch could be controlled without the use of hands. This criterion is related to the objective that students will apply their knowledge of electric circuits to real-life problems (which was our initial guess as to the underlying objective). Finally, the fourth criterion "looks at the students' description of how their switch works." This criterion is, in fact, related to the second objective—namely, that students will understand how a switch works to power and control a light, but with an added twist. Students must understand various ways to operate switches that do not involve touching them. (Note. All quotes were taken from www.pals.sri.com/tasks/5-8/ME122.rubric.html.)

The important point to be made here is that the evaluation criteria, not the task descriptions, are the means by which extended response tasks are

TABLE 4.3
Sample Problem-Solving Task

Your team has been hired to help remodel a house so people who do not have the use of their hands will be able to turn lights on and off. For the device to work, you will need to:

- make a circuit that conducts electricity
- design a switch to turn the circuit on and off
- adapt your design for people who do not have the use of their hands

Step 1. Make sure you can light a bulb.

Use the materials you have been given to create the circuit shown in the diagram.

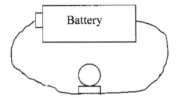

Does the light bulb light? If it does not, check to be sure that you have constructed the circuit properly, and ask your teacher to make sure that your bulb and battery are working.

Step 2. Build a switch.

Once the bulb in your circuit lights, use the materials you have been given to create a switch. Work with your switch until you can use it to turn the light bulb on and off. Add the switch to the circuit. When you have finished your drawing, return to your desk and answer the following two questions on a separate sheet of paper.

1. Draw your circuit and switch. Clearly label your drawing. Explain how the switch works.
2. Now figure out how you could change the design of the switch so that a person without the use of his or her hands could use it. Draw a diagram of your circuit showing the changes to the circuit and switch that would allow a person to turn it off and on without the use of hands. In your drawing, you must show all parts of the circuit and the switch. Each of the parts must be clearly labeled. Explain how this switch works.

Note. Adapted from www.pals.sri.com.

linked with the objectives. Thus, the objectives, tasks, and evaluation criteria must be considered simultaneously if sound and defensible extended response tasks are to be designed.

SCORING STUDENT RESPONSES TO EXTENDED RESPONSE TASKS

Tests comprised exclusively of selection and short-answer tasks are also referred to as *objective tests*. The correct or best response to each task is determined and placed on a scoring key. Everyone using the scoring key should arrive at the same score for each task, for each objective, and for the entire assessment for each student. In fact, the scoring key can be entered into an optical scan machine or a computer program, and the scoring can be done without humans being involved at all. The scoring key minimizes scoring errors and results in objective scoring.

Life is not so simple with extended response tasks. Someone has to read what was written (or drawn) or observe the actual performance. Based on this reading or observation, this person must assign one or more scores to what was written (or drawn) or performed to indicate whether or how well the student achieved the objective(s) being assessed. However, because there is no scoring key per se, we may not be confident that this person's assigned score(s) represents the student's actual achievement. Thus, we may decide to ask another person to read what was written (or drawn) or observe what was performed and, independently, assign his or her score(s). If both scores are identical (or nearly identical), we say we have a high degree of scorer or observer agreement. If the scores are quite different, we become concerned with the amount of subjectivity inherent in the score(s). We may bring in a third person to conduct yet another independent evaluation, or we may bring the two initial evaluators together to discuss and perhaps resolve their differences.

The likelihood of subjectivity entering into the scoring of extended response tasks is much greater when those doing the scoring have no guidelines to inform their scoring. Without guidelines, each scorer is left to his or her devices to determine what to consider (and what to leave out) and how well a student must do to get a certain number of points. To minimize subjectivity, some sort of guideline is absolutely essential. Three types of guidelines are used most frequently: checklists, rating scales, and rubrics.

Checklists

Scriven (2000) defined a checklist as a "list of factors, properties, aspects, components, ... or dimensions, the presence ... of which is to be separately considered, in order to perform a certain task" (p. 1). For the sake of simplicity, we use the term *criteria* to refer to all of the other items on Scriven's list. That is, criteria are the factors, properties, aspects, components, and dimensions used to evaluate something.

Checklists are valuable evaluation tools in several respects. A summary of their primary values is shown in Table 4.4. First, checklists are mnemonic devices. As a consequence, they reduce the chances of forgetting to consider something that is important. Second, checklists are easy to understand. As is seen later, they are much easier to understand than many rubrics. Third, like all evaluation procedures that include multiple independent criteria, checklists reduce the influence of the halo effect. The halo effect occurs when a general impression of the overall response or performance influences the scores given to individual elements of the response or performance. Fourth, checklists reduce the Roschach effect. This is the tendency to see what you want to see in a mass of data, rather than what is "really there." Fifth and finally, checklists are a way to organize knowledge to facilitate the accomplishment of certain tasks. We see this value of checklists as we explore them in greater detail.

Scriven identified several types of checklists. Three are the most relevant to our discussion: sequential checklists, criteria of merit checklists, and diagnostic checklists.

Sequential Checklists.   A sequential checklist is one in which the order in which the criteria are arranged is important. Students are expected or encouraged to meet the first criterion before moving to the second, the second before moving to the third, and so on. An example of a sequential checklist is shown in Table 4.5. This checklist is used to evaluate students' research projects. The six activities included in the checklist correspond with the way in which the research process is taught to students. That is, first they select topics. Next, they formulate questions. The last step is to present their findings. A checkmark is made in the "Completed?" column when the activity has

TABLE 4.4
Why Checklists Are Valuable

1.   Checklists are mnemonic devices.

2.   Checklists are easy to understand.

3.   Checklists reduce the influence of the halo effect.

4.   Checklists reduce the Roschach effect (i.e., tendency to see what one wants to see in a mass of data).

5.   Checklists organize knowledge to facilitate the accomplishment of certain tasks.

TABLE 4.5
Checklist for Evaluating Students' Research Projects

Activity	Completed?
Select topic for exploration.	
Formulate questions about selected topic.	
Identify potential sources of information.	
Gather information from a variety of sources.	
Employ a variety of strategies to prepare selected information.	
Present findings in a variety of finished products.	

been completed. It should be fairly obvious from this example that sequential checklists are useful in the assessment of objectives dealing with applying procedural knowledge. As might be expected, sequential checklists are generally associated with a reasonably high level of objectivity.

Criteria of Merit Checklists. Whereas a sequential checklist focuses exclusively on completing the steps in a process, criteria of merit checklists focus on the quality of the product that results. Consider, for example, the criteria of merit checklist used to evaluate students' answers to the Advanced Placement European History examination (Table 4.6). The checklist contains six criteria. For each criterion, the reader of the examination has to decide whether to assign a point to the student's answer.

In contrast to sequential checklists, criteria of merit checklists tend to be somewhat more subjective. Far more judgments are called for on the part of the person(s) doing the scoring. What is an "acceptable thesis statement?" How do I know that the student "understands the basic meaning of the documents?" To reduce this possible subjectivity, many criteria of merit checklists are converted into rating scales or rubrics as we shall see later.

Criteria of merit checklists can be used to assess a wide variety of objectives (e.g., understanding conceptual knowledge, applying procedural knowledge, evaluating based on factual and conceptual knowledge, creating based on all types of knowledge). The Evaluation Center at Western Michigan University provides a great deal of information about criteria of merit checklists, along with several examples. Their Web site address is www.umich.edu/evalctre/checklists.

Diagnostic Checklists. Diagnostic checklists are designed to aid in the identification of the cause of a problem. Diagnostic checklists are included in pamphlets and booklets accompanying a variety of electronic devices, such as computers, printers, DVD players, and so on, frequently

TABLE 4.6
Criterion of Merit Checklist for Scoring AP European History Examination

Criteria	Point Assigned?
1. Has an acceptable thesis statement	
2. Uses a majority of available documents	
3. Supports thesis with appropriate evidence from documents	
4. Understands the basic meaning of documents cited in essay (May misinterpret one document)	
5. Analyzes bias or point of view in at least two of the three documents	
6. Analyzes documents by grouping them in one (or two or three) ways depending on the question being addressed	

under the heading of "Troubleshooting." The message of the manufacturer is clear: "Before you call or write us, or before you return the machine to us, check these things." Is the machine plugged in? Are all the connections tight?

In education, diagnostic checklists permit us to go below the surface of the problem to explore potential causes or subproblems. Consider the diagnostic checklist shown in Table 4.7. The checklist is used to examine how students solve mathematical word problems. There are several reasons that students may arrive at the wrong solution to the problem. They may not recognize the problem type. They may conceptualize the problem all wrong. They may make computational errors. These reasons become the row entries in the diagnostic checklist.

Diagnostic checklists can be developed to help us understand learning problems of students in a variety of subject areas. Why does the student fail to understand basic concepts? Why does the student have difficulty applying learning to new situations? Why does the student not engage in metacognitive activities such as self-regulation? As might be expected, however, diagnostic checklists are not easy to develop since they must be grounded in reasonable explanations for the problem under investigation.

Rating Scales

It is a short hop from criteria of merit checklists to rating scales. Both require meaningful criteria that are directly related to the objectives being assessed. Unlike checklists that call for a presence/absence, yes/no, or checkmark/no checkmark response, rating scales require that a judgment of degree be made. How much? How often? How good? These are the ques-

TABLE 4.7
Diagnostic Checklist for Solving Mathematical Word Problems

Source of Difficulty	Present?
Did not recognize the type of problem it was	
Picture indicates some conceptual problems	
Did not differentiate relevant from irrelevant information	
Selected incorrect procedure to solve the problem	
Made one or more computational errors	
Did not check to see whether solution was reasonable (e.g., placement of decimal point, appropriateness of unit of measurement)	

tions that rating scales require. In simplest terms, then, a rating scale is a criteria of merit checklist with a 4-point, 5-point, or 6-point scale attached. Consider the rating scale displayed in Table 4.8.

The first four criteria correspond with four primary objectives pertaining to oral communication: using appropriate volume, pitch, rate, and tone; using proper gestures, eye contact, facial expressions, and posture; expressing ideas with fluency, elaboration, and confidence; and using props and other visual aids to enhance the performance. Based on students' performances, teachers can assign a rating of "5" (highest) to "1" (lowest) to each of these four criteria. If either of the two lowest ratings are assigned, written comments explaining the ratings are requested. The final criterion permits an overall evaluation of the performance. Whatever rating is given on this criterion, written comments are required. The written comments are intended to provide feedback that students can use to improve their performance.

Quite obviously, rating scales have the potential to substantially increase the subjectivity involved in scoring. To combat this potential problem, the use of anchors has been strongly recommended by several experts in the field. An anchor is a sample of student work that exemplifies one of the scale points. If you have five scale points (e.g., as in Table 4.8), you would have five anchors. For the rating scales in Table 4.8, the anchors could consist of short videotapes of scenes acted out by students. Each scene could be keyed to each of the criteria (e.g., "This is a '4' on volume, pitch, rate, and tone, but a '2' on using props and other visual aids to enhance the performance"). When designed and used properly, anchors provide meaning to the scale points associated with each criterion. Because of

TABLE 4.8
Rating Scale for Evaluating Play Performance

Directions. Rate the performance in terms of each of the following criteria. Circle a "5" if the performance was excellent in this area and a "1" if it was very poor in this area. Use the numbers in between as necessary and appropriate. Write a brief reason for giving either a "1" or "2" on any criterion.

1. Actors use appropriate volume, pitch, rate, and tone.   5   4   3   2   1
    Comments:

2. Actors use proper gestures, eye contact, facial ex-   5   4   3   2   1
    pressions, and posture.
    Comments:

3. Actors express ideas orally with fluency, elaboration,   5   4   3   2   1
    and confidence.
    Comments:

4. Actors used props and other visual aids to enhance   5   4   3   2   1
    the performance.
    Comments:

5. Overall evaluation of performance.   5   4   3   2   1
    Comments (required):

Note. From Spartanburg County (SC) School District Five.

this, anchors are essential to interrater agreement and, hence, should decrease the subjectivity involved in scoring extended response tasks. In fact, Wiggins (2000) cautioned against using alternative assessments if anchors are unavailable. In his words,

> Without anchors the assessment is incomplete at best and fatally flawed at worst: there will be a lack of inter-rater reliability since judges will be left to interpret the [criteria] in a vacuum, students will not be able to self-assess or understand the expectations, and local judges will not be able to justify their standards as being credible. (p. 2)

Rubrics

A rubric is a rating scale in which a verbal summary of each rating point is written. In analytic rubrics, there are rating scales associated with multiple criteria, each linked with a specific objective. In global rubrics, there is a single rating scale associated with a single, quite general criterion. Often this single criterion integrates a set of more specific criteria. As we see later, both analytic and global rubrics can be all purpose or may be developed specifically for a given task.

Global Rubrics.   Tables 4.9 and 4.10 contain examples of global rubrics. The rubric in Table 4.9 is an all-purpose rubric. That is, it can be used with a variety of extended response tasks in mathematics. In contrast, the rubric in Table 4.10 is a task-specific rubric. The assessment task was as fol-

TABLE 4.9
Example of an All-Purpose Global Rubric

Criteria	Points
The response accomplishes the prompted purpose and effectively communicates the student's mathematical understanding. The student's strategy and execution meet the content, thinking processes, and qualitative demands of the task. Minor omissions may exist, but do not detract from the correctness of the response.	4
The response provides adequate evidence of the learning and strategic tools necessary to complete the prompted purpose. It may contain overlooked issues, misleading assumptions, and/or errors in execution. Evidence in the response demonstrates that the student can revise the work to accomplish the task with the help of written feedback. The student does not need a dialogue or additional information.	3
The response partially completes the task, but lacks adequate evidence of the learning and strategic tools that are needed to accomplish the prompted purpose. It is not clear that the student is ready to revise the work without more instruction.	2
The response demonstrates some evidence of mathematical knowledge that is appropriate to the intent of the prompted purpose. An effort was made to accomplish the task, but with little success. Minimal evidence in the response demonstrates that with instruction the student can revise the work to accomplish the task.	1
The response lacks any evidence of mathematical knowledge that is appropriate to the intent of the task.	0

Note. From Colorado Department of Education (www.cde.state.co.us/cdeassess). Reprinted with permission.

TABLE 4.10
Example of a Task-Specific Global Rubric

Levels of Performance	Range of Points
Clear argument regarding question of reconciliation; sophisticated understanding of Lincoln's views on race and slavery; solid understanding of historical context of 1850s and 1860s (may emphasize one period); factual documentation may contain inconsequential errors	13–15
Addresses question of reconciliation; understands Lincoln's views on race, slavery; understands historical context of 1850s and 1860s; factual documentation may contain minor errors	10–12
Attempts to address question of reconciliation; discussion of Lincoln's views and historical context of 1850s and 1860s may be uneven; limited factual documentation; some errors	7–9
Little or no attempt to address questions of reconciliation; factual documentation may be irrelevant, inaccurate, confused; generalized discussion lacks substance; may contain major errors	4–6
Vague on question; evidence inaccurate, incompetent; an inept or inappropriate response	1–3

Note. From Relearning by Design, Inc. (www.relearning.org).

lows: " I am not, nor have ever been, in favor of bringing about in any way the social and political equality of the white and black races." How can this 1858 statement by Abraham Lincoln be reconciled with his 1862 Emancipation Proclamation?"

Table 4.9 illustrates two of the problems frequently associated with global rubrics. First, each category contains at least five implicit criteria: task accomplishment, understanding, strategies, execution, and content knowledge. Although a score of "4" indicates that all five criteria have been met and a score of "0" indicates that none has, the meaning of the middle three scores in terms of the five criteria is not clear. For example, where does lack of accomplishment, but good understanding, reasonable strategies, poor execution, and moderate content knowledge fit into the equation? Second, the rubric reinforces the need for anchors in generating and using rubrics. To fully understand each of the category descriptions, you would need to see one or two student work samples that exemplify that category. Short-hand notations without more complete text make informed judgments difficult. Consequently, objectivity is once again threatened.

The rubric in Table 4.10 also contains multiple criteria in each category (i.e., reconciliation, Lincoln's views on race and slavery, historical context, and factual documentation). However, the issue of reconciliation tends to be predominant. The scale moves in descending order from *clear argument* to *addresses question* to *attempts to address question* to *little or no attempt to address question* to *vague on question*. The range of points permits an adjustment to be made within each category to take the other four criteria into consideration. Once again, anchors would be of great help in clarifying each of the five levels of performance.

Analytic Rubrics. Tables 4.11 and 4.12 contain examples of analytic rubrics. Table 4.11 contains an all-purpose rubric pertaining to writing, whereas Table 4.12 contains a task-specific rubric (viz. learning to graph). In reviewing these two rubrics, note that the criteria implicit in the global rubrics are now explicit. There are six criteria in Table 4.11 and four in Table 4.12. Also notice that analytic rubrics (and rubrics in general) can take many forms. The format of Table 4.11 is similar to the formats of the two tables exemplifying global rubrics. In contrast, the format of Table 4.12 is a two-by-two table, where the verbal descriptions are included in the cells of the table.

Finally, notice how the criteria included in analytic rubrics mirror the objectives set forth by the teacher. In writing, for example, students are expected to learn to:

- fully develop their ideas, supporting them with details;
- write in an organized fashion;
- use vocabulary to get their ideas across to the reader;
- vary their sentence structure with no structural errors; and
- make few, if any, errors in capitalization, punctuation, and spelling.

Similar, although more specific, objectives can be inferred from the rubric shown in Table 4.12.

Because of this relationship between evaluation criteria and objectives, analytic rubrics provide useful information about student achievement on an objective-by-objective basis. Thus, when objective-by-objective information is needed to make a decision, analytic rubrics should be used. In contrast, in those cases where objectives focus primarily or exclusively on higher order cognitive processes that transcend individual objectives, global rubrics are preferable.

Teachers interested in designing rubrics are encouraged to visit www.rubistar.4teachers.org, www.teach-nology.com, and www.uni.edu/

TABLE 4.11
Example of All-Purpose Analytic Rubric

Criteria/Description of Ratings	Score
Ideas and Development	
Extensive development of topic; strong support of main idea with details	4
Good development of topic; many supporting details	3
Adequate development of topic; listing of details	2
Weak development of prompt; few or no details	1
Organization	
Completely organized; smooth flow with strong sequence	4
Fairly well organized; flow and sequence evident	3
Sparsely organized; lack of sequence	2
Not organized	1
Vocabulary	
Vivid and imaginative word choice; appropriate use of vocabulary	4
Good word choice; meaning is clear	3
Fair word choice; simple words	2
Poor or inappropriate word choice	1
Sentence Structure	
Excellent; no errors and a variety of lengths	4
Adequate; few errors and some variety of lengths	3
Fair; choppy with no variety	2
Poor; many errors	1
Capitalization and Punctuation	
Error free	4
Very few errors (1–5)	3
Some errors (6–10)	2
Many errors (over 10)	1
Spelling	
Error free	4
Very few errors (1–5)	3
Some errors (6–10)	2
Many errors (over 10)	1

TABLE 4.12
Example of Task-Specific Analytic Rubric

Criteria	Number of Points			
	4	3	2	1
Data table	Data in table are well organized, accurate, and easy to read	Data in table are organized, accurate, and easy to read	Data in table are accurate and easy to read	Data in table are not accurate and/or cannot be read
Type of graph	Graph fits the data well and makes them easy to interpret	Graph is adequate and does not distort data, but interpretation of data is somewhat difficult	Graph distorts the data somewhat and interpretation of the data is somewhat difficult	Graph seriously distorts data making interpretation almost impossible
Units	All units are described (in a key or with labels) and appropriately sized for the data set	Most units are described (in a key or with labels) and are appropriate sized for the data set	All units are described (in a key or with labels), but are not appropriately sized for the data set	Units are neither described nor appropriately sized for the data set
Accuracy of plot	All points are plotted correctly and easy to see. A rule was used to neatly connect the points or make the bars	All points are plotted correctly and easy to see	All points are plotted correctly, but are not easy to see	Points are not plotted correctly or extra points were included

Source: Rubistar.4teachers.org

93

profdev/rubrics. These sites allow teachers to either borrow or tailor make rubrics based on prototypes provided.

ANALYZING RESULTS OF EXTENDED RESPONSE ASSESSMENTS

In our discussion of analyzing the results of assessment instruments composed primarily of selection and short-answer tasks, I suggested that a two-dimensional table should be prepared. The table rows would correspond with individual students, and the table columns would correspond with individual assessment tasks. In the case of extended response assessments, I once again suggest that a two-dimensional table be prepared. Furthermore, the rows would still correspond with individual students. However, the labeling of the columns would change based on the type of scoring guideline used.

If checklists are used, then the columns would correspond with the criteria included on the checklist. In terms of the diagnostic checklist (Table 4.7), for example, the table would include six columns, with each column corresponding with a particular source of difficulty. A "1" would be placed in a cell if a particular student had that particular difficulty, whereas a "0" would be placed if he or she did not.

Data from rating scales and rubrics can be treated similarly. The difference would be between global rubrics (and rating scales), on the one hand, and analytic rubrics (and rating scales), on the other. For global rubrics, the column labels would correspond with the possible point values. On a four-point scale, for example, the table would include four columns, one labeled "1," one labeled "2," and so on. Each student would have a "0" in three of the columns and a "1" in the column corresponding with his or her score on the global rubric. By reading down the columns you would be able to calculate the number of students scoring "1," "2," and so on.

For analytic rubrics, the column labels would correspond with the criteria. So if, as in Table 4.11, you have six criteria, you would have six columns (Ideas and Development, Organization, Vocabulary, Sentence Structure, Capitalization and Punctuation, and Spelling). In this situation, the numbers in the cells would represent the scores each student received on each criterion with, using the rubric in Table 4.11, scores ranging from 1 to 4. By summing the rows, you would get a total score across all criteria for each student. By summing the columns, you would get a total score for each criterion. Differences in these column scores would indicate the criteria on which students did the best and those on which they did the worst.

ASSIGNING SCORES TO STUDENTS

When we considered selection and short-answer tasks, I suggested that individual student scores should be assigned after problematic tasks were eliminated. Because of the few numbers of extended response tasks typically included, this is generally not an option. Rather, student scores should be assigned directly from the tables mentioned earlier. Modifications in the assessment tasks, if needed, would affect the next generation of students.

CHAPTER FIVE

Assessing Student Classroom Behavior and Effort

> For most teachers no assessment activity is more pervasive than the informal observation of student behavior. Teachers constantly look at students and listen to what is occurring in the class. (McMillan, 1997, p. 107)

As mentioned several times previously, the primary method of assessing student classroom behavior and effort is observation. As McMillan (1997) suggested, these observations are typically informal, meaning that the "observation is unstructured in the sense that there is no set format or procedure" (p. 108). At the same time, however, informal observations do have a focus and purpose. Actually, there are two general purposes. The first is to gather information to make instructional decisions (e.g., Should I speed up or slow down? Should I stop talking and move to an activity that will wake them up a bit?). These observations have a group focus. The second purpose is to identify individual students who may be having difficulty and need more attention or a different venue. Obviously, these observations have an individual student focus. For these students, a movement to more formal observations may be necessary as more specific and precise information becomes warranted.

There are times when teachers need to go beneath what they see and hear to understand more fully what they observe. In the terminology introduced in chapter 1, they need to move beyond description of student behavior to search for explanations for it. This chapter begins with a discussion of informal observation. We then move to a discussion of more formal observation. Finally, the issue of what lies beneath the surface of what teachers see and hear is addressed.

INFORMAL OBSERVATIONS

One of my favorite research findings concerning classroom management is that teachers, in general, are not good at managing classrooms once "all hell has broken loose." Rather, teachers who are better classroom managers are simply better at not allowing this to happen (Emmer & Evertson, 1981). How do they do this? What knowledge and skills do teachers possess that enable them to, as Barney Fife would say, "nip it in the bud?"

Kounin (1970) came up with a partial answer to this question over 30 years ago. He called it *withitness*. During whole-class instruction, teachers who are *with it* maintain direct eye contact with their students. Yet even when not directly looking at their students, they are able to sense what is going on. In the vernacular, they seem to have "eyes in the back of their heads." During seatwork activities, they frequently scan the classroom to verify task engagement and locate children who may need assistance. When working with a small group, they continue to be aware of the rest of the class. Equally important, when they sense trouble brewing ("I could see it in the look in his eyes"), they move to stave it off without interrupting the flow of the classroom activity. For example, they may move physically closer to a student who is whispering to a friend while continuing to address the whole class. In this way, a potential disruption does not become an actual one. In summary, teachers who are *with it* are simply better *readers* of their students, and this *reading* is done almost exclusively on the basis of information obtained during informal observations.

Reading Nonverbal Behavior and Vocal Cues

You ask a question and look around the classroom. Many students are waving their hands eagerly. What do you conclude? Students are confident that their answers are correct. Sometime later you notice that students start to look around the room and at each other. What do you conclude? Some students may not understand what you are saying or they may be bored with your talking. You give students a written assignment to complete at their seats. You notice that most students get right to work. What do you conclude? Most students understand the assignment—both the material included on it and what they need to do to complete it.

All of these conclusions are based on information collected during informal observations. All teachers rely a great deal on facial expressions, body language, and vocal cues (i.e., how something is said, not what is said) to get information about their students. Yet the fact remains that some teachers just read their students better than others. That is, the conclusions they draw from the information they receive are simply more accurate. How can teachers improve their reading? Three answers to this question are discussed in the following sections: teachers can understand the message, they can focus their attention, and they can seek a different perspective.

Understand the Message

McMillan (1997) linked facial expressions, body language, and vocal cues with the messages they convey. Nine different messages are included in Table 5.1. The first three—confident, happy, and interested—are positive messages. For example, when a student is interested, he or she makes direct eye contact, leans forward in his or her seat, and talks more rapidly in a slightly higher pitched voice. These are the kind of messages teachers like to receive from their students. No changes need to be made.

The last six messages—angry, bored, defensive, frustrated, nervous, and not understanding—are negative messages. For example, when a student

TABLE 5.1
Messages Students Convey Through Nonverbal Behavior and Vocal Cues

Message	Facial Expressions	Body Language	Vocal Cues
Confident	Relaxed; direct eye contact	Sitting up straight; hands waving; forward position in seat	Fluent; few pauses; variety in tone; loud
Happy	Smiling; smirking; eyebrows natural	Relaxed; head nodding; leaning forward	Animated; fast; loud
Interested	Direct eye contact; eyebrows uplifted	Leaning forward; nodding; raised hand or finger	Higher pitched; fast
Angry	Eyebrows lowered and drawn together; teeth clenched	Fidgety; hands clenched; head down	Loud or quiet; animated
Bored	Looking around; relaxed	Slumped posture; Hands to face	Soft; monotone; flat
Defensive	Downcast eyes; eyes squinted	Arms and legs crossed; leaning away; head on hands	Loud; animated
Frustrated	Eyebrows together; downcast eyes; eyes squinting	Tapping; picking; placing fingers or hands on each side of head	Pauses; low pitch
Nervous	Eyebrows lowered	Rigid; tapping; picking	Pauses; repetition; shaky; soft; quiet; fast
Not Understanding	Frowning; biting lower lip; eyes squinting; looking away	Leaning back; arms crossed; head tilted back; hand on forehead; scratching chin; leaning head on hands	Slow; pauses; low pitch; monotone; quiet; soft

Note. From McMillan (1997).

is frustrated, he or she has downcast eyes, taps his or her fingers or pencil on the desk or places his or her fingers or hands on each side of the head, and speaks with frequent pauses in a lower pitched voice. Teachers would rather not receive these messages because the implication is that something needs to change.

Teachers who are good readers of their students are not only keen observers of behavior, but they are able to understand the messages these behaviors convey. Consequently, they are able to differentiate a student who is frustrated from one who is bored, a student who is angry from one who is defensive. These are important distinctions to make.

Focus Your Attention

It is difficult to simultaneously observe 20 or 30 students in a classroom. Reducing the number of students in your perceptual field generally produces more reliable information. In this regard, I am reminded of an interview I had with a 7-year-old on the topic of smaller class sizes. He had been in a class of 26 students in first grade and was currently in a class of 15 students, the result of a district-wide class reduction policy. After I asked what he liked best about being in a smaller class, I asked if there things he did not like about it. He paused for a moment and then said: "There's no place to hide." Teachers tend to be more aware of each and every student in smaller classes. What can be done in larger classes?

In chapter 1, the concept of *steering group* was introduced. As a reminder, a steering group is a relatively small group of students in the classroom (perhaps four or five) whose reactions the teacher relies on to make decisions concerning the pacing of instruction. This concept can be expanded to include other decisions. Suppose, for example, students are working on a written assignment at their desks. As you monitor your steering group, you notice that all but one is having difficulty with Question 5. Do you continue to work with each individual student or do you reconvene the whole class and go over Question 5 together? Clearly, the whole-class decision is superior from an efficiency point of view. Similarly, as you talk to your class, suppose you notice that the majority of your steering group members is bored to the point of almost falling asleep. It is time to do something else.

The composition of the steering group should reflect the type of decision you intend to make based on the information that you gather. For example, there are students in almost every classroom who are more visible in terms of the social structure of the group. That is, other students watch these students for cues about what to do and what not to do; what is permissible and what is not; what rules can be bent and which cannot. A decision about whether to stop the lesson and intervene in a case of misbehavior and when to simply ignore the misbehavior and continue with the lesson would be well informed by having these socially visible students as members of the steering group. If the behavior in question is exhibited by one of the steering group members, it may be wise to intervene. The reason for doing so would be to stop what Kounin (1970) referred to as the *ripple effect* (i.e., the spread of the behavior from student to student, much as the ripples of water when a rock is thrown into a pond).

Using steering groups is one way to reduce the observational load placed on teachers in larger classes, thereby increasing the validity and reliability of the information obtained from informal observations. Another approach is to stop periodically and reflect on the information you obtained from informal observations of each student over time. The use of a rubric, such as the one shown in Table 5.2, or a rating scale, such as the one shown in Table 5.3, can make this reflective time more productive. Both the rubric and rating scale are simple and quite straightforward. The criteria on both are those of the greatest importance to most teachers. Concerns for classroom behavior and effort are key components of both the rubric and rating scale.

Completing the rubric or rating scale serves three purposes. First, each provides a written record of behavioral strengths and weaknesses that can be shared with students and their parents on a periodic basis. Communication of assessment results is a critical step in using them constructively and productively. Second, having a written record is important if there is a need to move beyond informal to more formal observations. More is said about this transition from informal to formal observations later in this chapter. Third, the process of completing the rubric or rating scale can provide the teacher with insights as to which students are getting lost in the shuffle. Not all students are equally salient in the perceptual world of the teacher. Some early research indicated that two groups of students were the most salient in the eyes and minds of most teachers: the *stars* and the *problem children*. Quiet, unassuming, so-called *average* students are often overlooked. If, while completing the rubric, you find that you are not sure whether Ida comes prepared to class or makes contributions to the class discussion, this may suggest the need to pay more attention to Ida during your informal observations over the next few days or weeks.

Seek a Different Perspective

Evertson and Green (1986) compiled a list of the sources of error in informal observation. Many of these errors stem from the lens through which a teacher looks at his or her students and his or her classroom. Examples include:

- Primacy effects (where teachers' initial impressions have a distorting effect on subsequent observations);

TABLE 5.2
Rubric for Class Participation

Criteria	Point Values			
	4	*3*	*2*	*1*
Attendance/promptness	Student is always prompt and regularly attends classes.	Student is late to class no more than once every 2 weeks; regularly attends classes.	Student is late to class more than once every 2 weeks and/or skips a class or two.	Student is late to class more than once a week and/or frequently skips class.
Preparation	Student is almost always prepared for class with assignments and required materials.	Student is usually prepared for class with assignments and required materials.	Student is rarely prepared for class with assignments and required materials.	Student is constantly unprepared for class with assignments and required materials.
Behavior	Student almost never displays disruptive behavior during class.	Student rarely displays disruptive behavior during class.	Student occasionally displays disruptive behavior during class.	Student constantly displays disruptive behavior during class.
Level of engagement	Student contributes to class by offering ideas and asking questions on a regular basis.	Student occasionally contributes to class by offering ideas and asking questions.	Student rarely contributes to class by offering ideas and asking questions.	Student never contributes to class by offering ideas and asking questions.

Source: teachers.teach-nology.com

TABLE 5.3
Rating Scale for Student Classroom Behavior

Criteria	Good	Fair	Poor	NA
Accepts responsibilities				
Arrives on time and follows rules				
Comes prepared for class				
Completes assignments on time				
Contributes to class discussion				
Makes an effort to learn				
Makes good use of time				
Works well with others				

Note. From Boreson (1994). N/A means "not applicable"

- Logical generalization errors (where teachers make the assumption that what he or she observes in one situation is likely to apply in other situations);
- Failure to acknowledge self (where teachers do not take into account the influence they have on the setting or situation and the resultant student behavior);
- Observer bias (where preconceived biases and stereotypes distort the meaning of what is observed); and
- Student faking (where teachers fail to notice that students appear to behave in accordance with teacher expectations, but are not).

There are two ways to deal with these errors. The first is simply to be aware of them. As the old saying goes, "Knowing is half the battle." The second is to routinely seek out those who have potentially different perspectives. There are two groups whose perspectives may be of particular value to the teacher: their students and their colleagues.

Student Perspectives. Simple checklists can be used to gather information from students about their classroom behavior and effort. One example is the checklist shown in Table 5.4. The statements on the checklist range from those dealing with paying attention (Items 1 and 6) to those dealing with effort (Items 2 and 3) to those dealing with understanding (Items 4, 5, 7, and 8).

The checklist can be given to students several times a semester or year. In this way, changes over time can be noted. It is strongly recommended

TABLE 5.4
Student Involvement Checklist

Directions. Read each statement below, thinking back over today's lesson. If you agree that the statement expresses something that you thought or did during the lesson, place a checkmark in the "YES" column. If you believe that the statement does not, place a checkmark in the "NO" column.

Item	Description	YES	NO
1	I paid attention almost the whole time in class today.		
2	If I didn't understand something, I just gave up.		
3	I tried very hard to learn what the teacher was teaching.		
4	Nothing we talked about seemed to make sense to me.		
5	I tried to connect what we were learning to what I already knew.		
6	During class my mind often wandered.		
7	I think I could explain what I learned today to other students.		
8	I had trouble understanding what we were talking about.		

Note on scoring: For odd-numbered statements, YES responses are worth 1 point, whereas NO responses are worth 0 points. For even-numbered statements, the reverse is true. The total number of points is computed and the higher the total score, the greater the student involvement.
From Anderson (1991).

that students respond anonymously (Popham, 1994). Although this makes it impossible to link responses to individual students, anonymity increases the validity of the data for the group or class of students assessed. By looking at the overall responses given by students, teachers know, for example, how may students "paid attention almost the whole time today" or "tried very hard to learn" what he or she was teaching. These results can be compared with the teachers' perceptions of how the lesson went. In this way, differences between teacher and student perspectives can help the teacher become a better reader of his or her students.

Colleague Perspectives. In everyday life, it is extremely difficult to be concerned simultaneously about what you are saying and doing and what other people are saying and doing. If you get very involved in what you are saying, you often become unaware of how those around you are reacting to what you are saying. Conversely, the more you are aware of those around you, the more difficulty you may have in deciding what to say. So it is with classroom teachers. It is difficult to think about your teaching and think about how students are reacting to your teaching while you are teaching. To ameliorate this problem, you can invite a colleague into your classroom. Simply stated, colleagues provide another pair of eyes (and ears). At the same time, however, you want those eyes (and ears) to be focused. Structured observation forms, such as the one shown in Fig. 5.1, are intended to provide that focus.

Prior to the observation, your colleague provides the information called for at the top of the form (date, beginning time, and number of students in the classroom). Then every 5 minutes, your colleague does a scan of the classroom. During this scan, he or she determines where each student falls into the six status categories: on-task, mind elsewhere, socializing, misbehaving/classroom rules, aggressive, or out of room. Generally speaking, the colleague focuses on the latter five categories first. Those students not obviously falling into one of these off-task categories are assumed to be on task. Mind elsewhere includes daydreaming, sleeping, and the like. Misbehaving/ classroom rules indicates that only behavior that is counter to your classroom rules should be counted. Finally, aggressive behaviors can be either verbal or physical.

Each student is placed into one of the six categories every 5 minutes. The simplest way to do so is to have your colleague use tallies as he or she scans the room (i.e., II for two, III for three, etc.). Near the end of each 5-minute period, your colleague should ask, "Based on what I have observed, where does each student belong in terms of the classification system?" Obviously students may vary in their behavior from minute to minute. If this becomes a problem, the time span can be shortened from 5 to 1 or 2 minutes, with multiple pages used for a single observation period.

Quite obviously, your colleagues are busy people. They may not have time to observe in your classroom. One way to solve this problem is to take turns observing in each other's classrooms. In this way, peer observation becomes a part of the cultural expectations of the school. Another way to solve the problem is to use trustworthy teacher aides or parent volunteers. The structured observation form included in Fig. 5.1 requires only a general knowledge of classroom expectations and student behavior. Consequently, in a short period of time, teacher aides and parents can be trained to use the form with quite valid and reliable results.

FROM INFORMAL TO FORMAL OBSERVATIONS

In the overall scheme of things, the phrase *formal observations* can be equated with *documentation*. That is, formal observations are needed pri-

Date	Beginning Time		Number of Students in Classroom							
		Time Segments (Five-Minute Periods)								
Status of Student	A	B	C	D	E	F	G	H	I	J
On Task										
"Mind Elsewhere"										
Socializing										
Misbehaving/Rules										
Aggressive										
Out of Room										
Total Off-Task										

FIG. 5.1   Classroom profile on student behavior. Adapted from Squires, Huitt, & Segars (1983).

marily when a teacher is leaning toward a decision about an individual student and needs documentation to support, defend, or justify that decision. Three examples of these decisions are:

- talking with parents about a recurrent problem with their child's behavior, effort, or achievement;
- referring a student for counseling; and
- recommending that a student be considered for placement in special education.

Formal observations differ from informal observations in three important ways. First, they must yield more precise information. Second, when using formal observations, the behavior or behaviors must be examined over time and across different settings. Third, formal observations are usually part of highly structured information-gathering and decision-making procedures.

The Need for Increased Precision

Earlier I mentioned that information obtained from rubrics (see Table 5.2) and rating scales (see Table 5.3) could be useful as you move from informal to formal observations. Although they are useful in this regard, the information obtained from these rubrics and ratings scales still lacks the precision required of formal observation. From an informal observation perspective, "arrives on time and follows rules" is sufficient. From a formal observation perspective, however, we would need to know when and how many times the student was late and how often and what rules the student failed to follow. Thus, although informal observations can rely on categories of behavior, formal observations must result in the documentation of specific instances of the categories.

It should be clear from this example that when moving from informal to formal observation, the focus shifts from describing what a student does and does not do to documenting what a student does improperly or does not do. Thus, formal observations tend to have a decidedly negative bent. The reason for this, plain and simple, is that the information from formal observations is used most frequently to justify a forthcoming "negative" decision or recommendation. If your decision or recommendation is called into question, you need precise data to support it.

The Need for Stability

In addition to increased precision, there is a need with formal observations to document the consistency or persistence of the problem behavior. Consistency or persistence enables teachers to argue that the source of the problem resides in the student, not in the environment. This distinction corresponds with the long-held psychological differentiation between *trait anxiety* and *state anxiety*. Trait anxiety is anxiety that is a characteristic (trait) of a person. Simply stated, some people are more anxious than others. In contrast, state anxiety is a characteristic of the environment. Some situations or settings (collectively *states*) are more anxiety producing than others. (Obviously, a sadist would enjoy placing a highly anxious person in an anxiety-producing setting, thereby killing two birds with one stone).

If a student consistency misbehaves in Mr. Kaasa's class, but does not misbehave at all in Mr. Herzog's, this raises the possibility that Mr. Kaasa may be part of the problem. However, if the student misbehaves in both classes, it is more likely that the source of the behavioral problem resides within the student. Similarly, if a student works hard learning the lyrics of a hip hop song, but does not even attempt to memorize the periodic table of elements, this suggests that the student can put forth effort when he or she wants to do so; he or she just does not want to put any effort into chemistry. However, if neither hip hop nor chemistry nor anything else for that matter "turns the student on," we may be dealing with a student-based problem.

In the psychological and special education literature, *chronic* and *pervasive* are synonyms for stable. For example, the following behaviors are associated with attention deficit hyperactivity disorder (ADHD): difficulty concentrating, easily distracted, poor organizational skills, acting before thinking, and needing constant supervision. For a student to be classified as ADHD, however, these behaviors must be "chronic (present throughout the child's life), pervasive (present throughout the day), and are not due to other factors such as anxiety or depression" (Weiner, 1994, p. 55). All of us have difficulty concentrating or we act before we think from time to time. This does not mean that we have an entire population of ADHDs.

Before talking with parents, referring a student for counseling, or recommending a student for special education, it is incumbent on the teacher to ensure that the problem truly resides in the student. Partly because of this responsibility, teachers are expected to engage in *prereferral interventions* prior to referring a child for special education. "When a child is referred without appropriate pre-referral information (i.e., a preschool child or a parent referral), the evaluation planning process should address modification and adaptations to the various natural and learning environments" (North Dakota Department of Public Instruction, 1999, p. 10).

In other words, efforts must be made to eradicate the problem, and the effect of these efforts must be negative (i.e., the problem remains) before a student can be placed into a category or classification from which he or she is unlikely to escape. Stability of information is the key to solving the person–environment paradox.

The Need for Procedural Integrity

In addition to increased precision and high levels of stability, formal observation also requires that proper procedures be followed. These procedures are highly structured, often carrying the effect of law, regulation, or policy. Figure 5.2 contains a procedure that outlines the steps involved in referring a child for special education placement.

Teachers are typically involved early in the process (Step 1) and often are involved as members of the multi-disciplinary team (Step 4). The North Dakota State Department of Public Instruction (1999) described the role of the regular classroom teacher in the referral process in the following terms:

> The child's classroom teacher will provide vital information concerning the child's level of functioning within the general education curriculum and the instructional implications that result from the disability. The team depends on the classroom teacher for reporting classroom data such as the outcomes of diagnostic teaching, interactions with other students, and day-to-day performance. (p. 13)

There are (or certainly should be) clear procedures for referring students for counseling and special education placement. To ensure that each child is properly placed (or not placed), informal observations must give way to formal observations. This is the moral (and increasingly legal) responsibility of the classroom teacher.

MOVING BELOW THE SURFACE

Observations, whether they are informal or formal, have one major limitation. They can only describe what happens or fails to happen. They cannot help us explain why things do or do not happen. Why is Bethany misbehaving in class? Why does Grant never turn in any work? Based on our observations, we know that Bethany is, in fact, misbehaving and that Grant, in fact, never turns in any of his work, but we do not know why. To get below the surface, we need to focus on attempting to explain what we observe. To do that, we often have to rely on other sources of information. Before we know what information we need, we must explore the causes of the problems that we observe.

Explanations as Causal Models

In chapter 1, we discussed briefly the problem confronting Alfred Binet. Binet, you might remember, attempted to explain why some of the students in the French education system were failing. As we see later, he was

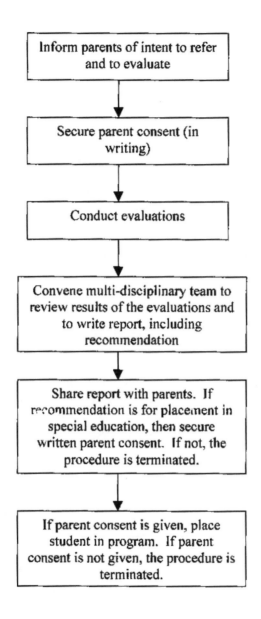

FIG. 5.2   A procedure for referring a student for special education placement.
Note. Members of the multi-disciplinary team should be "qualified professionals who
have expertise in the student's suspected disability and who can evaluate and determine the student's needs" (Boreson, 1994, page 4). Multi-disiplinary teams are also
known as Building Level Support Teams (BLST) (North Dakota Department of Public
Instruction, 1999).

not asked to explain why the French education system was failing some of its students. Rather, both Binet and the French Minister of Education assumed that the cause of student failure resided within the students. In other words, Binet operated within a rather simple causal model as shown in Fig. 5.3. According to this model, students failed either because they lacked the ability to succeed or were not motivated to succeed.

An alternative model for explaining school success and failure is shown in Fig. 5.4. In this model, school success can be attributed to either personal or environmental characteristics. That is, either Harvey lacks the ability to understand the material being presented in class or the teacher is so confusing that no amount of ability would allow Harvey to figure it out. Similarly, either Harvey is "just plain lazy" or the class is "god awful boring." Notice that both explanations produce the same observable result. Harvey doesn't do well in class, and Harvey does not turn in his assignments. Notice also that Binet's causal model is embedded within the model shown in Fig. 5.4. Both ability and motivation are personal characteristics. Because Binet was not asked to determine why the French education system was failing its students, it is not surprising that environmental factors were excluded from his causal model.

So what does this history lesson have to do with teachers' observations of students' classroom behavior and effort? Teachers are rarely content to simply describe what they see and hear. They often (and quite quickly I might add) move from description to tentative causal attributions: "… because Jimmy doesn't have any friends," "… because Jolene comes from a dysfunctional family," "… because Justin just likes to see me flustered," "… because Jerilyn doesn't have any confidence in herself." The word *because*

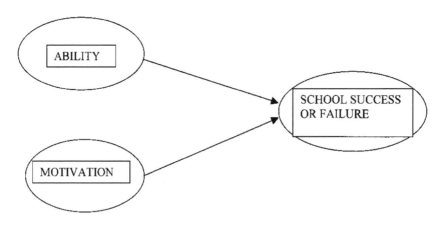

FIG. 5.3   Casual model linking ability and motivation to school success.

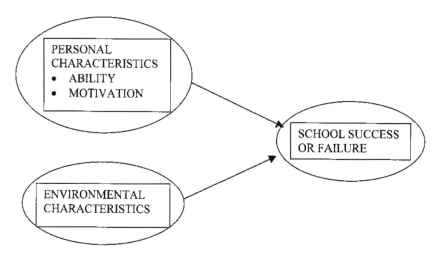

FIG. 5.4 Casual model linking personal and environmental characteristics with school success.

generally follows the question "Why?" The question "Why?" signals the search for an explanation. Thus, like Binet, most teachers are busy constructing causal models to help them explain what they see and hear. Teachers are unlike Binet, however, in two important respects. First, they are a bit more casual about causality. That is, they typically do not consider a variety of possible causes, opting instead for the first reasonable explanation that comes to mind. Second, teachers rarely systematically test the validity of their causal explanations. Rather, they consider them self-evident truths until something happens to convince them otherwise.

What is needed to improve teacher decision making in this area, then, is (a) considering alternative causes, resulting in a tentative causal model; and (b) subjecting the tentative causal model to empirical testing. Consider a teacher who has a student, Guillermo, who is in constant motion during the seatwork portion of the lesson, stopping periodically to talk quietly with a few students. His motion is distracting to the teacher and Guillermo's fellow students. The teacher's reasoning might go something like this: "I wonder why Guillermo can't sit still. Is it because he is ADHD? Is it because his breakfast consists of donuts and cokes and he has a 'sugar rush' in my first period classroom? Is it because he wants to socialize, so he moves around to talk with his classmates? Is it because the material I am teaching is too easy for him and he finds the seatwork assignment boring?" This set of questions produces the causal model shown in Fig. 5.5.

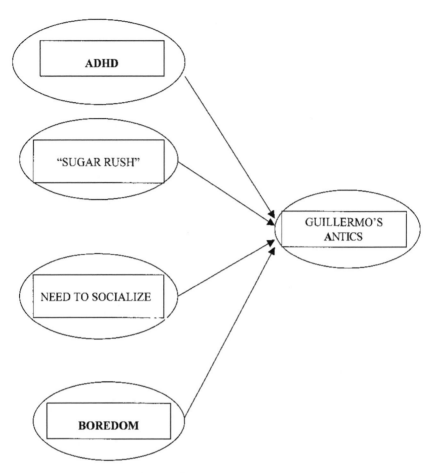

FIG. 5.5   Attempt to explain Guillermo's antics.

How do we decide which of the possible causes is the real one? Perhaps there are multiple causes as there often are when human behavior is examined. Basically, we proceed via a process of elimination:

• We began by gathering information about each of the possible causes of the problem. Because ADHD requires a judgment to be made by professionals, it would be the last possibility to consider. We are then left with the need to gather information about "sugar rush," "need to socialize," and "boredom." "Sugar rush" is easy because we only have to ask Guillermo what he generally eats for breakfast. Because "need to socialize" and "boredom" both fall into the category of "affective assessment," some type of affective assessment instrument, such as a survey or questionnaire, could be administered.

- After gathering information on each of the three probable causes, we examine the information. Suppose, for example, Guillermo does not eat sugar-laden breakfasts and is not bored by the material covered in class. However, he expresses a great need to socialize with his classmates.
- Based on this information, we attempt a simple intervention with Guillermo. Specifically, we say to him, "If you stay in your seat for the entire class period today, I'll set aside some time tomorrow for you to work with your friends." If Guillermo stays put, voila! If not, it may be necessary to consider the ADHD option with everything that entails.

This process of identifying a problem, determining possible causes, gathering information, intervening based on probable cause, and gathering additional information to see if the intervention worked lies at the heart of functional behavioral assessment (FBA; O'Neill et. al., 1997; Sugai, Lewis-Palmer, & Hagan, 1998). FBA is an integral part of the Individuals with Disabilities Education Act (IDEA; North Dakota Department of Public Instruction, 1999).

Table 5.5 contains a diagnostic checklist that supports FBA. The checklist contains four questions:

- Which of these problem behaviors has the student exhibited?
- How frequently does this student exhibit the problem behavior(s)?
- What events seem to trigger the problem behavior(s)?
- Why do you think the student is engaging in the problem behavior(s)?

In light of our previous discussion, the first question identifies the problem. The second addresses the stability of the problem behavior. The third question raises the possibility of environmental causes. The fourth asks about causes that reside within the student. By including both the third and fourth questions, FBA operates within the context of the causal model displayed in Fig. 5.4. That is, both environmental and personal causes are considered. As a consequence, the contents of the checklist can be displayed in causal model form as shown in Fig. 5.6. In Fig. 5.6, the problem behaviors are listed in the oval to the right. The response options for the third question have been summarized and listed under "Environmental Characteristics," and the response options for the fourth question have been listed under "Personal Characteristics."

The initial selection of one or more entries in the Environmental Characteristics and Personal Characteristics ovals depends on teachers' recollections of informal observations. At this point in the process, teachers have two options. They can assume that their causal explanations are reasonably

TABLE 5.5
Functional Behavioral Assessment (FBA) Diagnostic Checklist

Please take a few minutes to fill out this sheet. Your input will help us identify how we can help [name of student] behave better in school.

Which of these problem behaviors has the student exhibited in your classroom?

_____ Disruptive	_____ Unresponsive
_____ Fighting/physically aggressive	_____ Vandalism
_____ Inappropriate language	_____ Withdrawn
_____ Insubordination	_____ Work not done
_____ Tardy	_____ Other _____
_____ Theft	

How frequently does this student exhibit the problem behavior(s) in your classroom?

_____ Less than once a week

_____ A few times a week

_____ Once a class period

_____ Several times per class period

_____ Constantly

What events seem to trigger the problem behavior(s)?

_____ Poor or failing grades	_____ Physical demands
_____ Activity too long	_____ Physical proximity to peers
_____ Comment from peer	_____ Structured activity
_____ Correct/reprimand	_____ Unstructured time
_____ Tasks too difficult	_____ Tasks too boring

Why do you think the student is engaging in this problem behavior/these problem behaviors?

_____ To avoid an adult	_____ To avoid a peer
_____ To avoid a physical task	_____ To avoid failure
_____ To get adult attention	_____ To get peer attention
_____ To get something he/she wants	_____ To get out of academic work
_____ To get to do an activity	

Note. Adapted from Tobin (1994).

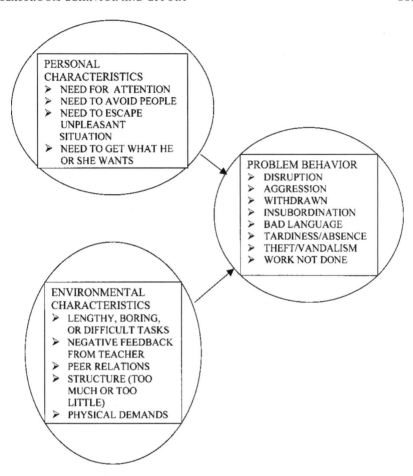

FIG. 5.6   Causal model based on FBA diagnostic checklist.

valid and move directly to the intervention stage (e.g., avoid providing any type of negative feedback to the student for a week, assuming that negative feedback from teacher is a major cause of the problem). Alternatively, they can elect to gather additional information about their causal explanations (for the purpose of corroborating their hypotheses) and then move to the intervention phase. One source of information is the students—a source that generally falls under the heading of *affective assessment.*

THE ROLE OF AFFECTIVE ASSESSMENT

Lists such as those shown in Table 5.5 help teachers formulate initial causal models. They get teachers to think through various possibilities before arriving at their interpretations of students' classroom behavior and effort. An alternative approach, however, is to use causal models that already have been developed. This approach has several advantages. First, the models are research based (i.e., they have developed over time as researchers have systematically studied the problems). Second, because the models are research based it is fairly easy to tie them directly to existing affective assessment instruments. Third, although the models are research based, they tend to make sense to teachers (as we see later). Thus, by being aware of these models in advance, teachers can avoid rediscovering the wheel. In this section, two such models are considered, the first related to effort and the second related to classroom behavior. Although there are other models, the two to be discussed meet all three criteria mentioned previously: They are research based, they can be connected to affective assessment instruments, and they are sensible to teachers.

Understanding a Lack of Effort

In chapter 1, the expectancy-value theory of motivation was described briefly. It is now time to consider it in greater detail. The theory can be expressed as a causal model as shown in Fig. 5.7. As its name suggests, expectancy and value are the two primary constructs in the model. *Expectancy* can be defined as the degree to which a student expects to be successful. *Value* can be defined as the degree to which success is important to the student. This question can be asked, however: "Success in what?" The simple answer is "success in school"; that is, learning what is expected to be learned and/or receiving grades indicative of learning success.

As shown in Fig. 5.7, expectancy of success on a new learning task or, quite possibily, on an entire set of learning tasks that define a subject area (e.g., mathematics) is a function of three interrelated factors. They are prior successes (or failures), self-efficacy ("I can or can't learn it"), and locus of control ("If I work hard I can learn" vs. "It doesn't matter how hard I work, I still can't learn it"). The value attached to a new learning task or, quite possibility, an entire set of academic tasks also depends on three interrelated factors. They are aspirations ("I want/don't want to get as much education as I can"), perceived importance or use ("I care/don't care if I learn this stuff. I see/don't see how it can help me"), and interests ("This is really cool/boring").

As mentioned, these are interrelated factors as a couple of examples show. A student who has received failing grades in mathematics through his or her entire elementary school career is required to take 7th-grade mathematics. It is safe to say that this student has experienced little, if any, success in learning mathematics. Consequently, he or she truly believes he or she cannot learn mathematics. Furthermore, he or she believes that no

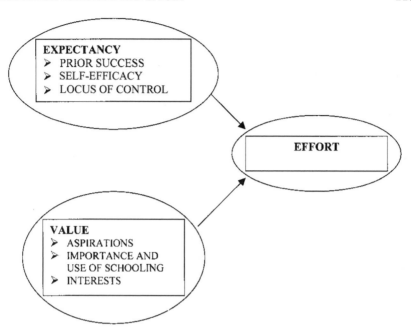

FIG. 5.7   Casual model based on expectancy-value theory of motivation.

amount of effort will produce mathematics achievement. One would expect this student to be the proverbial unmotivated mathematics student. Why should we expect otherwise? Similarly, a student does not see education is his or her future plans and believes that what is being taught in school is boring and irrelevant. Like the former student in mathematics, this student is likely to be regarded as unmotivated. Unlike the former student, however, this lack of motivation may transcend learning tasks and subject matters, being generalized to formal education as a whole.

To identify the cause(s) of an individual student's lack of effort, then, we have to gather information about these various factors. Because we have limited the factors to six in the entire model, this is not an impossible task. In fact, a diagnostic assessment battery could be prepared rather easily, with all of the information gathered in a relatively short period of time (say, 1.5 or 2 hours). Prior success can be estimated from the grades received by the student.

Table 5.6 has been prepared to aid in the selection of instruments to include on an affective assessment battery. The top half of the table contains two instruments for each of five affective characteristics: self-efficacy, locus of control, aspirations, importance and usefulness of schooling, and inter-

TABLE 5.6
Examples of Affective Instrument for Potential Causes
of Misbehavior and Lack of Effort

Affective Characteristic	Instrument and Source
Self-efficacy	Situational Confidence Questionnaire [Kirisci & Moss, 1997] Motivated Strategies for Learning Questionnaire: Self-Efficacy Scale [Pintrich, Smith, Garcia, & McKeachie, 1991]
Locus of control	Locus of Control Scale for Children [Nowicki & Strickland, 1973] Intellectual Achievement Responsibility Scale [Crandall, Katkovsky, & Crandall, 1965]
Aspirations	Student Aspirations Survey [Plucker, 1996] NELS 88 Aspirations Questions [Bradby, 1992]
Importance and usefulness of schooling	Life Roles Inventory—Achievement Value Scale [Fitzsimmons, Macnab, & Casserly, 1985] Motivated Strategies for Learning Questionnaire: Task Value Scale [Pintrich, Smith, Garcia, & McKeachie, 1991]
Interests	Interest in Mathematics [Schiefele & Csikszentmihalyi, 1995] Interest in Foreign Languages [Gardner & MacIntyre, 1993]
Affective Characteristic	Instrument and Source
Sense of belonging	Psychological Sense of School Membership [Goodenow & Grady, 1993] Alienation Scale [Jessor & Jessor, 1977]
Classroom cohesiveness	My Class Inventory [Fraser, Anderson, & Walberg, 1982] Classroom Environment Scale [Moos & Trickett, 1987]

ests. In general, the assessment of interests is subject specific. Consequently, the two instruments included in the table focus on interest in mathematics and foreign languages. However, the format of these instruments can be used to assess interest in other subject areas as well as interest in specific tasks (e.g., science experiments, mathematical word problem, British novels).

It is important to note that the vast majority of these instruments are appropriate for middle and high school students. A few can be adapted for upper elementary school students. In general, listening to students—either in naturalistic settings or in brief arranged conversations with the teacher—is probably the best way to gather this affective assessment information from elementary school students. For example, if a third-grade student constantly says, "I can't! I can't! I can't!," this would suggest a problem with self-efficacy.

Understanding Problem Classroom Behavior

Fig. 5.8 contains a model of what has been called the *process of disengagement* (Finn, 1989). It begins with a lack of a sense of belonging. The student comes to believe he or she is not welcomed, respected, or valued by others in the school community—students as well as teachers. In a word, he or she does not *belong*. He or she begins to feel alienated and anonymous. Once this feeling sets in, the student is likely to decrease his or her participation in school and classroom activities. Conflicts are more likely to arise between student and others. Absenteeism increases and grades decline. As a result, the student is likely to be suspended or even expelled, which simply reinforces the belief that he or she does not belong in the school. Eventually, the student leaves school on his or her own (Osterman, 2000). As Roderick (1993) stated quite succinctly: "Dropping out ... is an act of rejecting membership in a community in which youths feel marginal, gain little self-esteem, perceive few rewards, and which they experience as rejecting them" (p. 82). It is important to note that a feeling of belonging eventually impacts on all three major areas: classroom behavior, effort, and achievement.

One of the keys to understanding classroom behavior problems, then, lies in understanding a student's sense of belonging. A related factor is how cohesive the student sees his or her classroom as being. Affective assessment instruments related to both sense of belonging and classroom cohesiveness are included in the bottom two rows of Table 5.6. The "My Class Inventory" is appropriate for elementary school students, whereas the "Classroom Environment Scale" is appropriate for high school students.

Also with younger school-age children, parents who report that their children constantly complain about having to go to school, perhaps even to the point of tears, may have very useful information on the early stages of the process of disengagement. With this early identification, intervention plans involving both parents and teachers would have a greater likelihood of success.

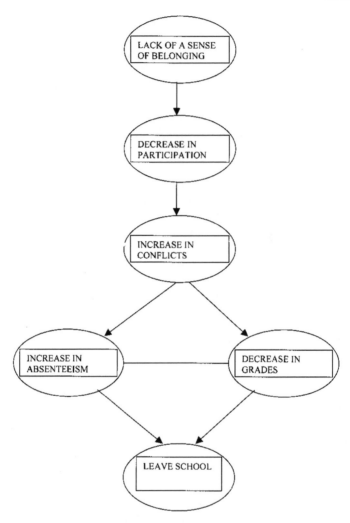

FIG. 5.8   The process of disengagement.

Informal Affective Assessment Instruments

Just as teachers construct their own instruments to assess student achievement, it is possible for them to construct their own instruments to assess affective characteristics. In fact, the procedure outlined in chapter 3 is
similar to the procedure for constructing affective assessment instruments, although a bit shorter. To construct affective assessment instruments, I recommend a five-step procedure.

The first step is the preparation of a blueprint. This blueprint is similar to that for a student achievement assessment instrument made up exclusively of selection tasks. The stem is generally a complete sentence, and the response options are variations on those included in the traditional Likert scale (*strongly agree, agree, undecided, disagree, strongly disagree*).

The second step is to actually write the statements. In writing the statements, the following guidelines should be kept in mind:

- Ensure that each statement involves opinions and feelings and cannot be construed as a statement of fact.
- Keep the language of the statements simple, clear, and direct.
- Write statements in the present tense (i.e., how students feel now).
- Ensure that each statement contains only one complete thought.
- Avoid words that are vague modifiers or may not be understood by students asked to complete the instrument.
- Avoid statements that involve double negatives (what does it mean to strongly disagree with a negatively worded statement?).

The third step is to write the directions. Fig. 5.9 contains three examples of directions. The first is for an instrument dealing with perceived importance (hence, value). The second is for an instrument dealing with self-perceptions (e.g., self-efficacy). The third is for an instrument dealing with classroom cohesiveness. These are useful models for writing your own directions.

The fourth step is to have your draft instrument reviewed. Your colleagues and students are both useful in this step. Your colleagues can focus on the structure of the instrument per se. Your students can focus on word choice, sentence structure, and clarity of directions. You may want your students to review it after they have had a chance to actually complete the instrument. In this way, you can watch them to see what observable difficulties they are having, as well as to determine about how much time is needed to administer the instrument.

The fifth step is to prepare a final draft of your instrument. In preparing this draft, you should make whatever changes are needed based on the feedback you received from your colleagues and students. In addition, the instrument should look as professional as possible. That is, it should look as if a person who truly cared about what students thought and felt prepared it. Finally, the instrument should be as short as possible while providing sufficiently reliable data for you to make the decision(s) you need to make.

Before moving to the next chapter, one final point must be emphasized. The purpose of affective assessment in this chapter is to help teachers gain a deeper understanding of their students in terms of the classroom behavior and effort. As a consequence, affective assessment instruments,

For each of the following statements, indicate how important it is to you. Use the following scale:

       1 means of little of no importance.

       2 means of some importance.

       3 means important and

       4 means very important.

Use a pencil to circle the number that shows how important the statement is to you. For example, if it is important for you to do well in school, you would fill in the answer sheet in the following manner:

    Doing well in school.   1   2 ③ 4

Read each of the following sentences. If you think the sentence is very true of you, circle 6; if the sentence is not true of you at all, circle 1. If the sentence is more or less true of you, choose a number between 1 and 6 that best describes you. Because only you know how you feel, there are no right or wrong answers. Just answer as accurately as possible.

I would like to know how you really feel about being in this class. This is not a test, and there are no right or wrong answers. I just want you opinion. Your answers will not be seen by anyone else.

Each sentence on the next page begins with MY CLASS IS A PLACE WHERE. Then you will read something that may happen to you or a feeling that you have. You should give your opinion by checking one of the boxes in each line to show that you agree, mostly agree, mostly disagree, or disagree with the sentence. Try to give an answer to every sentence, but if you really cannot decide just skip that one.

FIG. 5.9 Examples of generic directions for affective scales.

whether selected or designed, must be linked to one or more constructs included in a model that attempts to explain problematic classroom behavior or a serious lack of effort on the part of students. The two causal models included in this chapter are useful in this regard, but are not necessarily the only models. What is important, however, is that the selection or development of a causal model must precede the selection or design of affective assessment instruments. In this way, the construct validity of the affective assessment instruments is likely to be enhanced.

CHAPTER SIX

Interpreting Assessment Results

Throughout this book, I have emphasized the importance of making sense of the information you gather by means of classroom assessment prior to making any important decision. For example, the use of anchors gives meaning to the points included on rating scales and rubrics. Similarly, the use of causal models enables you to understand a classroom behavior problem or a student's lack of effort. In the context of classroom assessment, *making sense, giving meaning,* and *understanding* can be considered synonyms. Another synonym, one more directly associated with classroom assessment, is *interpreting.*

The purpose of this chapter is to explore three ways in which assessment information pertaining to individual students can be interpreted: by making comparisons with an underlying continuum, by making comparisons with other students, and by making comparisons with some preset standard(s). Note that all interpretation involves some type of comparison. Furthermore, different comparisons will likely yield different interpretations. Because of this last point, this chapter ends with a discussion of the need for multiple comparisons.

As an introduction to these three ways of interpreting assessment information, suppose that Erik is a high school wrestler and is concerned about his weight. He steps on his bathroom scale and reads "120." He interprets this number in terms of a continuum of pounds. He can make this interpretation because he knows that his weight in measured in pounds (not stones or kilograms), and that the assessment instrument is calibrated in pounds. Because Erik is a wrestler, however, he has another basis for interpreting "120"—namely, the continuum of weight classes. He knows there are 14 weight classes, with upper limits of 103, 112, 119, 125, 130, 135, 140, 145, 152, 160, 171, 189, 215, and 275. Relative to these weight classes, he would fall into the fourth lowest weight class (i.e., from 120–125 pounds). Both of these interpretations—one relative to pounds and the other relative to weight classes—are examples of interpretations based on comparisons with an underlying continuum.

Erik can also interpret his weight in terms of his schoolmates. He knows that he is one of the lightest boys in the junior class, well below the average weight of all juniors. His weight is also well below that of the average member of the wrestling team. Currently there are 27 boys on the wrestling team, with an average weight of 152 pounds. Only three of the boys on the wrestling team are lighter than he is. All of these interpretations are made based on comparisons with other students. In fact, two different groups of students are used to make the comparisons: high school juniors and members of the wrestling team. In the terminology of assessment, these are called *normative samples, norm groups*, or, my preference, *reference groups*.

Finally, suppose that Erik has a great desire to wrestle in the 113- to 119-pound weight class. This desire leads to our third type of comparison. The weight class "113 to 119 pounds" becomes the preset standard that Erik will use to interpret his weight. Based on this comparison, he understands that he is one pound over weight. Notice that if he were interested in wrestling at the 120- to 125-pound weight class, his interpretation would likely be just the opposite. He would be a little underweight and could stand to gain a few pounds.

Each of the following sections in this chapter focuses on one of these three types of interpretations. They are discussed in the order illustrated before—comparisons made with an underlying continuum, comparisons made with other students, and comparisons made with preset standards. This roughly corresponds with the order in which these three types of interpretations arrived on the education scene.

COMPARISONS WITH AN UNDERLYING CONTINUUM

In chapter 4, we discussed rating scales. Specifically, we mentioned that, unlike checklists, rating scales require that judgments of degree be made. How much? How often? How good? In the context of our current discussion, each rating scale constitutes a continuum. This continuum may be quantitative; like weight, the differences along the continuum are differences in amount. The questions "How much?" and "How often?" require a quantitative continuum. A continuum may be qualitative; like beauty, the differences along the continuum are differences in kind. The question "How good?" requires an underlying qualitative continuum.

It is instructive to point out that the term *scale* is derived from the late Latin word *scala*, meaning ladder or staircase. In assessment, a scale is, in fact, a ladder, with each rung indicating an increase in amount or quality. In addition to weighing scales, people are familiar with temperature and musical scales. The Merriam-Webster Dictionary defines a *musical scale* as a "graduated series of musical tones ascending or descending in order of pitch according to a specific scheme of their intervals" (www.m-w.com). Like musical scales, scales used for assessment purposes must possess a "specific scheme of their intervals."

The earliest recognized assessment scale was developed by E. L Thorndike (1910). It consisted of 16 handwriting samples arranged in order from least to most legible. During the assessment process, students were asked to write a few specified sentences. To evaluate the handwriting of a particular student, the sentences written by the student would be compared with the various handwriting samples. Eventually, the handwriting sample most closely resembling the sentences written by the student would be determined, and the score assigned to that sample would be assigned to the student's handwriting.

Scales were a key component of most of the assessments developed during the early 1900s. In addition to the Thorndike Handwriting Scale, there was the Willing Scale (for elementary school written compositions), the Hudelson English Composition Scale (for secondary school narrative compositions), and the Harvard-Newton scales (which covered not only narration, but also description, exposition, and argumentation; Pressey & Pressey, 1922). The Presseys' noted that the Hudelson English Composition Scale is "presented in a booklet, together with directions, norms, and (an admirable feature) a set of compositions on which the teacher may practice rating; these samples have been graded by expert judges so that she may check up her ratings by comparison with the values assigned by these experts" (p. 101).

The astute reader may notice the similarity between these various scales and the concept of *anchor* discussed in chapter 4 and mentioned previously. An anchor, in fact, is a set of examples arranged on an underlying continuum. The examples define the specific scheme of the intervals on the continuum, thereby giving meaning to the key points along the continuum. The verbal descriptions included on rubrics are but short-hand notations.

With extended response assessment tasks, the interpretive continuums underlie the criteria used to score students' responses to the tasks. The tasks are structured so that the students respond in ways that enable their responses to be scored using the developed criteria. As mentioned in chapter 4, these criteria (not the tasks) are the embodiment of the objectives set forth by the teacher.

Selection and Short-Answer Tasks

When selection and short-answer tasks are used in assessment, it is the tasks **not** the scoring criteria that embody the objectives. Therefore, if comparisons with an underlying continuum are to be used to interpret the results of these assessment task forms, care must be taken to arrange the assessment tasks along some underlying continuum.

To illustrate this point, we use examples taken from the National Adult Literacy Survey (NALS; Barton, 1994). In preparation for the survey, NALS researchers prepared 166 selection and short-answer tasks representing three types of literacy: prose, document, and quantitative. In conducting the NALS, more than 400 trained interviewers visited nearly 27,000 homes during the first 8 months of 1992. Each survey participant responded to only a sample of the 166 tasks, although all three types of literacy were represented in each sample of tasks. The survey took just over an hour to complete, 45 minutes to complete the assessment tasks, and another 15 to 20 minutes to provide demographic data.

Based on the responses of all 27,000 participants, the researchers placed the 166 tasks on a continuum of difficulty. Easier tasks (i.e., those answered correctly by a large number of participants) were placed at the lower end of the continuum, whereas harder tasks (i.e., those answered correctly by a small number of participants) were placed at the upper end of the continuum. Separate continuums were then developed for each of the three types of literacy, and each continuum was divided into five categories (Level 1–Level 5), much like the five points on a rating scale.

Rather than compute a total score, a profile of correct and incorrect responses was prepared for each participant. Examples of two profiles are shown in Table 6.1. Notice that Participant A performed the six easiest tasks correctly, but did not perform any of the more difficult tasks correctly. Thus, in terms of literacy, Participant A would be placed between Levels 2 and 3. However, Participant A tends to exist only in an ideal world. Because assessment is imperfect, Participant B has a more realistic profile. Note that Participant B got the three easiest correct, but missed Task 4. He got the next three tasks correct, then missed three in a row. Inexplicability, he got Task 11 correct and then missed the four most difficult tasks. If we focus on the five categories, however, the general pattern of Participant B is quite similar to that of Participant A. Consequently, when all of the responses are considered, Participant B would also be somewhere between Levels 2 and 3 in terms of literacy.

How can these patterns of responses be used to aid interpretation? When assessment tasks and student responses can be placed on the same scale (as in the earlier weighing example or as shown in Table 6.1), it becomes possible to interpret a student's performance in terms of the underlying continuum. Consider our two imaginary participants in Table 6.1. If we were to summarize these participants' performances, we would conclude that they probably can perform tasks at Levels 1 and 2, but they cannot perform tasks at Levels 3, 4, and 5. By analyzing these tasks in terms of their learning expectations (i.e., objectives), we can come up with descriptions such as those

TABLE 6.1
Continuum of Task Difficulty and Participant Profiles

	Level 1			Level 2			Level 3			Level 4			Level 5		
Continuum of task difficulty	T1	T2	T3	T4	T5	T6	T7	T8	T9	T10	T11	T12	T13	T14	T15
Participant A profile	R	R	R	R	R	R	W	W	W	W	W	W	W	W	W
Participant B profile	R	R	R	W	R	R	R	W	W	W	R	W	W	W	W

Note. T1 through T15 represent 15 tasks arranged in order of difficulty, where T1 is the easiest and T15 is the most difficult. An R in the cell indicates a right answer, a W in the cell indicates a wrong answer. Finally, Level 1 indicates the lowest level of literacy, whereas Level 5 indicates the highest.

shown in Table 6.2. These verbal descriptions are, in fact, interpretations of what we learned from surveying these two participants.

Can classroom teachers use this approach to interpret student assessment results? Generally, yes. In chapter 3, it was suggested that a two-dimensional table (Table 3.6) could be used to analyze students' responses to determine the quality of an assessment instrument and make modifications to improve the instrument as necessary. A similar two-dimensional table can be used to aid in the interpretation of student's scores on the assessment instrument. Table 6.3 displays a slightly reorganized version of

TABLE 6.2
Interpreting Literacy Using an Underlying Continuum

Participants A and B Probably CAN:	*Participants A and B Probably CAN'T:*
Locate a single piece of information when there is distracting information or other information that seems plausible but is incorrect. Compare, contrast, or integrate two or more pieces of information within a single, relatively simple, passage (e.g., underline the meaning of a term given in a government brochure; interpret instructions from an appliance warranty statement)	Integrate or synthesize information from complex or lengthy passages and make more complex inferences (e.g., state in writing an argument made in a lengthy newspaper article; compare two metaphors used in a poem).
Locate a single piece of information with distracting information present or requiring a low level of inference. Integrate information from various parts of the document (e.g., locate an intersection on a street map; determine eligibility from a table of employee benefits).	Integrate several piece of information from one or several documents and deal with rather complex tables or graphs that contain information that is irrelevant or inappropriate to the task (e.g., identify information from bar graphs depicting sources of energy and years; enter information given into an automobile maintenance record).
Perform a simple arithmetic operation using numbers given in the task or easily located in the material such as an order form (e.g., calculate postage and fees for certified mail; determine the difference in price between tickets to two Broadway shows).	Perform tasks where two or more numbers are typically needed to solve the problem and the operations must be determined from the arithmetic relation terms used in the question or directive (e.g., use calculator to calculate differences between regular and sale price from an advertisement; calculate miles per gallon using information given on a mileage record chart).

Note. Adapted from Barton (1994).

TABLE 6.3
Summary of the Results for 18 Students Completing a 20-Item Test

Objective	I	V	I	II	III	II	II	V	III	V	V	III	V	I	I	IV	IV	III	IV	III	
Student / Task Number	1	12	8	2	11	16	10	15	18	14	6	17	20	13	5	4	19	3	9	7	RT
Vernon	1	1	1	1	1	1	1	1	1	1	1	1	1	1	1	1	1	1	1	1	20
Felicia	1	1	1	1	1	1	1	1	1	1	1	1	1	1	1	1	1	1	1	1	20
Wells	1	1	1	1	1	1	1	1	1	1	1	1	1	1	1	1	1	1	1	0	19
Kitty	1	1	1	1	1	1	1	1	0	1	1	1	1	1	1	1	1	1	0	0	17
David	1	1	1	1	1	1	1	0	1	0	1	1	1	1	1	1	1	1	1	0	17
Michael	1	1	1	1	1	1	1	1	1	0	1	1	1	1	1	1	0	0	1	0	16
Jordan	1	1	1	1	1	1	1	0	1	0	1	1	1	1	1	1	0	1	1	0	16
Jackson	1	1	1	1	1	0	1	1	1	1	1	1	1	1	1	1	0	0	0	0	15
Janice	1	1	1	1	1	1	1	1	1	1	1	1	1	1	1	0	0	0	0	0	15
Alice	1	1	1	1	1	1	0	1	1	1	1	1	1	1	0	0	0	1	0	0	14
Betty	1	1	1	1	1	1	0	1	1	1	1	1	1	1	0	0	1	0	0	0	14
Steve	1	1	1	1	1	0	1	1	1	1	1	0	0	0	0	0	1	0	0	0	11
Connie	1	1	0	1	1	1	1	1	1	1	1	0	0	0	0	0	0	0	0	0	10
Jody	1	1	1	0	1	1	1	1	1	1	0	1	0	0	0	0	0	0	0	0	10
Merrill	1	1	1	1	0	1	1	1	1	1	0	0	1	0	0	0	0	0	0	0	10
Becky	1	1	1	1	1	1	1	1	1	1	0	0	0	0	0	0	0	0	0	0	10
Russ	1	1	1	1	1	1	1	1	0	0	0	0	0	0	0	0	0	0	0	0	8
Mike	1	1	1	1	1	1	0	0	0	0	0	0	0	0	0	0	0	0	0	0	6
CT	18	18	17	17	17	16	15	15	15	13	13	12	12	11	9	8	7	7	6	2	

Note. This table is not identical to Table 3.6. Modifications have been made for instructional purposes.

129

Table 3.6. As in Table 3.6, the students are arranged in order from the highest scoring to the lowest scoring. The columns of the table have been rearranged, however. Specifically, the tasks are now listed in the order of difficulty, from the easiest to the most difficult. Each task remains linked to an objective as shown by Roman numerals in the top row of the table. Finally, the incorrect response options shown in Table 3.6 have been replaced by zeros, indicating an incorrect response.

To provide a bit more substance to the example, let us assume that the five objectives were included in a middle-school unit on literary devices. More specifically,

- Objective 1 deals with understanding the concept of alliteration,
- Objective 2 deals with understanding the concept of personification,
- Objective 3 deals with understanding the concept of simile,
- Objective 4 deals with understanding the concept of metaphor, and
- Objective 5 deals with using literary devices to improve one's writing.

As shown in Table 6.3, there are three tasks associated with Objectives 1 and 2, four tasks associated with Objectives 3 and 4, and six tasks associated with Objective 5.

Because the items are arranged from easy to difficult, there should be a string of 1s from left to right. Unless a student gets a perfect score, the string is eventually broken by a 0. After the 0, in an ideal world, there would be no additional 1s. That is, when the string of 1s ends, this should indicate the students achievement level. For visual clarity, the initial string of 1s for each student is shaded in the table. The expected pattern is a diagonal rising from the lower left of the table to the upper right. Except for Jackson, Janice, Betty, and Steve (for whom the shaded portion is a bit shorter than expected) and Alice, Connie, and Jody (for whom the shaded portion is a bit longer than expected), the expected pattern holds fairly well.

A "1" following a zero indicates a student who should not have responded correctly to a more difficult task given that he or she missed one or more easier ones, but he or she did. The three most likely explanations for these errors in the patterns are (a) objective-specific knowledge, (b) guessing, and (c) flaws in the tasks. For example, Alice, Betty, and Steve unexpectedly responded correctly to Task 19 (Objective 5). They also unexpectedly responded correctly to Task 13 (Objective 3, understanding similes). Betty and Steve also unexpectedly responded correctly to Task 18 (Objective 3, understanding similes). Alice also responded correctly to Task 18, but it was not unexpected given her earlier pattern of responses. Suppose for the sake of argument that Task 19 requires an application of the concept of *simile*. If so, then one possible conclusion to be drawn is that Alice, Betty, and Steve understand the concept of simile, better than several of the other students in the class. This is an example of objective-specific knowledge.

Given that the pattern holds reasonable well, what interpretations can be made? A relatively simple interpretation is shown in Table 6.4a. Because the three easiest tasks were aligned with the first objective, and because all but one of the students responded correctly to these three tasks, we can conclude that students with total scores of at least three have mastered the first objective. The fourth and fifth easiest tasks are aligned with the second objective. However, because Task 16 aligned with fifth objective is the sixth easiest task, we have to move to the seventh easiest task to incorporate all three tasks aligned with the second objective. Thus, we can conclude that students with total scores of at least seven have mastered the second objective (as well as the first). We continue in the same way to produce the minimum scores associated with the mastery of the third, fourth, and fifth objectives.

It should be noted that we have applied a conservative definition of *mastery,* in that a student has to respond correctly to all tasks aligned with an objective to be said to have mastered the objective. We could loosen this definition a bit, saying, for example, that for Objectives 3, 4, and 5 a student could miss one task and still have mastered the objective. Table 6.4b was prepared based on this somewhat more liberal definition.

As in the case of the adult literacy example, Tables 6.4a and 6.4b can be used to interpret students' scores. With a total score of 14, Betty quite likely understands the concepts of *alliteration, personification*, and *simile*, but has some difficulty with the concept of *metaphor* and the application of literary elements in writing. Similar statements can be made for all students from Kitty down to Alice. From a group-based perspective, virtually all of the students exhibited an understanding of *alliteration* and *personification*. Several (from Connie or Steve on down) had problems with *simile*; the majority of the class exhibited at least some difficulty with *metaphor* and the application of literary elements to writing.

Affective Assessment Tasks

Most affective assessment instruments are composed of one or more scales. That is, students respond to affective assessment instruments by, in fact, placing themselves along a continuum. Consider the classic Likert scale response options. The continuum ranges from *strongly disagree* to *strongly agree*, with *undecided* in the middle. Anderson and Bourke (2000) suggested that this underlying continuum can be used to interpret students' scores on Likert scales. If we assign a value of 1 to *strongly disagree* and a value of 5 to *strongly agree*, our underlying continuum ranges from 1 to 5, with 3 as the neutral point. Regardless of the number of tasks

TABLE 6.4a
Interpretation of Student Scores Based on Placement
of Underlying Continuum

Student's Scores	Interpretation
3 or more correct	Student understands concept of alliteration
7 or more correct	Student understands concept of personification
14 or more correct	Student understands concept of simile
19 or more correct	Student understands concept of metaphor
20 correct	Student is able to apply literary elements in writing

TABLE 6.4b
Interpretation of Student Scores Based on Placement
of Underlying Continuum

Student's Scores	Interpretation
3 or more correct	Student understands concept of alliteration
7 or more correct	Student understands concept of personification
11 or more correct	Student understands concept of simile
17 or more correct	Student understands concept of metaphor
18 or more correct	Student is able to apply literary elements in writing

included, you can always return to this scale by dividing each student's total score by the number of tasks. For example, suppose an affective assessment instrument contains six tasks and a student receives a total score of 23 points. Twenty-three divided by 6 is 3.83.

A score of 5 would place a student at the positive end of the continuum, whereas a value of 1 would place him or her at the negative end. If our positive end represents a strong effort–achievement link, whereas our negative end represents a weak effort–achievement link, we can create a range around the neutral point, perhaps one half of a point, to indicate a moderate effort–achievement link. Each student can then be placed into one of the three categories based on his or her score: strong effort–achievement link, moderate effort–achievement link, and weak effort–achievement link. Furthermore, for group data, it is possible to indicate the number and percentage of students who fall into each of these three categories along the continuum.

COMPARISONS WITH OTHER STUDENTS

One of the best examples of comparisons with other students is the computation of high school rank. Students are ranked from 1 to n (where n is the number of students in the graduating class) on the basis of their grade point averages. Just to confuse matters a tad, lower numbers indicate higher ranks and higher numbers indicate lower ranks. Hence, a rank of 1 is as good as it gets. To help college admissions' committees better understand the high school rank of a particular student, the rank may be placed in the context of the total number of students in the graduating class. Thus "7/ 483" means that the student finished seventh in a graduating class of 483.

Not surprisingly, the word *rank* is part of the term *percentile rank*, which conjures up commercial norm-referenced tests. Norm-referenced tests are those designed in a way that the score(s) of one student can be interpreted by making comparisons with other students' scores. Consequently, one of the primary goals of the developers of norm-referenced tests is to differentiate reliably among students. Through a process of test design, item writing, field testing, and response analysis, a set of items is selected for inclusion on the final form of the test battery. Four criteria are used to determine which tasks make the final cut.

First, the items as a whole must conform to the test design blueprint. Table 6.5 shows a portion of the test design blueprint for the Stanford Achievement Test, Ninth Edition (i.e., Stanford 9). As can be seen, there are 84 items related to reading and 82 items related to mathematics. These items are distributed into subtests (e.g., vocabulary, mathematics: problem solving) and content clusters (e.g., synonyms, measurement). This structure is in place before any of the items are written.

Second, the items can be neither too easy nor too difficult. If all (or virtually all) students answer an item correct or incorrectly, that item is of no value in the overall scheme of things. Remember that one of the primary purposes of norm-referenced tests is to differentiate reliably among students. An item that everyone answers correctly (or incorrectly) does not differentiate at all.

Third, each item must differentiate between those students who did well on the entire test and those who did more poorly. Stated somewhat

TABLE 6.5
Structure of a Portion of the Stanford Achievement Test, Ninth Edition

Category	No. of Items
Total Reading	84
Vocabulary	30
Synonyms	16
Context	7
Multiple meanings	7
Reading Comprehension	54
Recreational	18
Textual	18
Functional	18
Initial understanding	10
Interpretation	24
Critical analysis	10
Process strategies	10
Total Mathematics	82
Mathematics: Problem Solving	52
Measurement	5
Estimation	6
Problem-solving strategies	5
Number and number relations	6
Number systems and number theory	4
Patterns and functions	3
Algebra	5
Statistics	4
Probability	5
Geometry	9
Mathematics: Procedures	30
Computation/symbolic notation	8
Computation in context	18
Rounding	4

differently, the top-scoring students overall should get each item right more often than the low-scoring students. This is an application of the concept of *item discrimination* mentioned briefly in chapter 3.

Fourth, the items as a set must complement each other in terms of the information they provide. A test composed of 50 identical items is still a one-item test (50 times over). Thus, each item must add a unique piece to the overall test. Statistically speaking, the responses made by students to pairs of items must be slightly positively correlated.

Largely because of the third and fourth criteria, the distribution of the results of a commercial norm-referenced test is predetermined. Practitioners have come to know this distribution as the bell curve or normal distribution. Statisticians know it as the Gaussian distribution. Because this distribution permits reliable comparisons to be made among students, it is extremely useful in the preparation of commercial norm-referenced tests. Coming full circle, one of the keys to norm-referenced interpretation is the percentile rank.

To understand percentile ranks, you have to think opposite from the way you think about high school ranks. As mentioned earlier, with high school ranks, lower numbers are better. With percentile ranks, higher numbers are better. A percentile rank of 99 is as good as it gets. In our previous high school rank example, a student who ranks 7 out of a class of 483 would have a percentile rank of 99. To calculate percentile rank in this instance, you would divide 7 by 483 (1.4), subtract the quotient from 100 (98.6), and then round up (99). A percentile rank of 99 means that (approximately) 99% of the students in his or her normative sample or reference group have a high school rank equal to or lower than this student.

Because the normal curve has known properties, it is possible to use these properties in interpretating test scores. To better understand this possibility, consider the normal curve as depicted in Fig. 6.1. As shown in the figure, the greatest number of students is clustered around the arithmetic average of the distribution (also known as the *mean*). As one moves away from the mean in either direction, the number of students decreases.

To aid in the interpretation of test scores using the normal distribution, statisticians developed nine categories. Over time, these categories came to be known as the *standard nine categories* or, more commonly, *stanines*. The categories were established so that 4% of the students fell into each of the lowest and highest categories, 7% of the students fell into the next lowest and highest categories, and so on, until 20% of the students fell into the middle category (or 5th stanine).

As can be seen in Fig. 6.1, there is a clear relationship between percentile ranks and stanines. If 4% of the students are to be placed in the lowest stanine, then the students in this stanine would have percentile ranks below four. Similarly, if 7% are to be placed in the next to the lowest stanine,

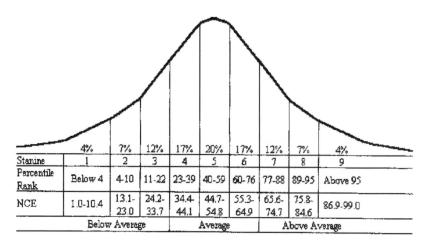

	4%	7%	12%	17%	20%	17%	12%	7%	4%
Stanine	1	2	3	4	5	6	7	8	9
Percentile Rank	Below 4	4-10	11-22	23-39	40-59	60-76	77-88	89-95	Above 95
NCE	1.0-10.4	13.1-23.0	24.2-33.7	34.4-44.1	44.7-54.8	55.3-64.9	65.6-74.7	75.8-84.6	86.9-99.0
	Below Average			Average			Above Average		

FIG. 6.1   The normal curve.

then the students in this stanine would have percentile ranks from 4 to 10. This link between stanine and percentile rank can be seen by examining the first and second rows under the normal curve in Fig. 6.1.

One problem with using percentile ranks in the context of the normal curve is that they tend to bunch up near the middle. At the tails of the distribution, each stanine contains only four percentile ranks. Near the middle of the distribution, however, a single stanine may include 17 or 20 percentile ranks. In an attempt to distribute students' scores more evenly along the normal distribution, the concept of normal curve equivalent (NCE) was born. NCEs are similar to percentile ranks with the notable exception that they are spread out more evenly along the normal distribution. As shown in Fig. 6.1, approximately 10 or 11 NCEs fall into each of the stanine categories.

As a historical note, NCEs were developed primarily to aid in the evaluation of the federally funded Title I program. A large proportion of students served by this program have very low scores on commercial norm-referenced tests. That is, they most often fall into the first or second stanines. Because of the unequal intervals of percentile ranks, students could get a lot more items right this year than last year and still not show any progress when the results were reported in terms of percentile ranks. Because NCEs are more evenly distributed across the normal curve, they are more sensitive to achievement gains made by students scoring at the lower tail of the distribution.

One aid to norm-referenced interpretation not shown in Fig. 6.1 is the use of quartiles. Quartiles are percentile ranks that divide the distribution into four quarters. Thus, the first quartile (Q1) corresponds with a percentile rank of 25. The second quartile (Q2) (also known as the median) corresponds with a percentile rank of 50. Finally, the third quarter (Q3) corresponds with a percentile rank of 25. Using quartiles, we can talk about students who are in the lowest quarter, next to the lowest quarter, next to the highest quarter, and highest quarter.

Quintiles and deciles are also reported and used in decision making. These are percentile ranks that divide the normative sample into 5 and 10 groups, respectively. To be eligible for enrollment in the Reading Recovery program (Clay, 1993), for example, students at some school sites must score at or below the lowest quintile (i.e., a percentile rank of 20).

Problems in Making Norm-Referenced Interpretations

There are three problems that teachers can encounter when attempting to make norm-referenced interpretations based on the results of commercial tests. The first concerns the phrase *grade equivalent*. The second is placing too much faith in the precision of the rankings. The third is not being aware of the composition of the normative sample or reference group.

Grade Equivalents.   The phrase *grade equivalent* has a specific meaning in the context of commercial norm-referenced tests. Grade equivalent scores are determined by administering a test developed for a particular grade level to students at other grade levels. For example, test designers prepare a fourth-grade test and then administer that test to second- and sixth-grade students. The key thing to remember here is that the test was intended to be a fourth-grade test. What does this mean? It means that the objectives on which the test was based are those appropriate for inclusion in the fourth-grade curriculum. From a statistical point of view, then, a second-grade equivalent score on this test is the average score of second- grade students on a test of fourth-grade objectives. Similarly, a sixth-grade equivalent score on this test is the average score of sixth-grade students on a test of fourth-grade objectives.

In light of this discussion, it should not be surprising that grade equivalent scores are often misunderstood. If a parent hears that his or her fourth-grade child has attained a grade equivalent score of 7.0 on some test, why shouldn't he or she think that the child belongs in the seventh grade? Because of the great possibility of contributing to misunderstanding and general confusion, grade equivalent scores should be reported and used with great caution. To properly interpret grade equivalent scores, you need to know about both the grade-level appropriateness of the tasks included on the test and the grade level of the students to whom the test was administered.

Insufficient Precision.   Going back to high school rank for a moment, it is interesting to note that in most high schools there is one valedictorian

and one salutatorian. Are we so sure that the differences between these two
students (as well as their classmates) are sufficiently large that we can reliably differentiate between and among them? (We could also ask whether we
are sure that high school rank is a valid measure of what it means to be successful in high school, but that is another matter.) An increasing number of
high school personnel apparently are not that certain. They have abandoned
the designation of *valedictorian* and *salutatorian* in favor of a group of ex-
ceptionally high achieving students (e.g., the top 10%).

The developers of commercial norm-referenced tests recognize the falli-
bility of students' scores on the tests. Consequently, they report percentile
rank bands, which take into consideration the various sources of error. The
lesson to be learned from this discussion is that the scores on which our
norm-referenced interpretations are based are not as precise as they seem
to be or as we would like them to be. This is not to suggest they are useless.
Error is inherent in all forms of assessment. Rather, this is to suggest that
they must be interpreted properly and used cautiously.

Composition of Normative Sample or Reference Group.   Because

students' scores are being interpreted relative to the scores of other students, it is essential to know something about the other students. In rare
cases, the normative sample is selected randomly from some well-defined population. Rather, commercial test publishers rely on school district administrators to volunteer their students to participate in the
testing program. Consequently, before a meaningful interpretation can
be made, several questions about the normative sample, norm group, or
reference group should be asked (and answered). Perhaps the most important question concerns the socioeconomic composition of the normative sample. There is a great deal of research linking socioeconomic
status (SES) to student achievement, particularly when data are aggre-
gated at the school and school district levels. Suppose, for example, 65%
of the students in your classroom qualify for free- or reduced-price
lunches. In contrast, only 30% of the students in the normative sample
qualify for free- or reduced-price lunches. You must ask yourself whether
comparing the achievement of your students with that of the normative
sample is a meaningful comparison.

One solution to this problem is to make comparisons with multiple
reference groups because each comparison contributes to our overall
understanding. Comparisons with students in the school, students in
the district, students in the state, students in the nation, students likely
to enroll in college, students likely to drop out of high school—all of
these have the potential to increase our understanding of the meaning
of students' scores.

COMPARISON WITH PRESET STANDARDS

There are standards, and there are standards. That is, there are standards that are virtually identical to objectives (as mentioned in chap. 1), and there are standards that indicate desired or expected levels of performance (as the term is used in this chapter). Many efforts have been made to minimize the confusion caused by using standards in two different ways. Some differentiate between content standards and performance standards; others, between standards and benchmarks. The focus of the discussion in this section is on the latter type of standards; that is, performance standards or benchmarks. When the term standard is used in this way, it suggests a dichotomy. Either a student has met the standard or he or she has not. The real issue in making comparisons with preset standards, then, is how to establish defensible standards.

Historical Standards

A student writes an essay that garners 94 points from his or her teacher. What grade should this student receive? An "A" obviously. How do we know? Because, historically, 94 has been used to divide the "As" from the "Bs." If we have used the standard in the past, how bad can it be? After all, courts throughout our land have used historical precedent to justify a number of their decisions.

Arbitrary Standards

In many ways, historical standards are somewhat arbitrary. If they were meaningful at one time, we have forgotten why they were. In modern times, arbitrary standards can be illustrated by the current zero-tolerance policies governing weapons in schools. Within the context of this policy, steak knives can be considered weapons, and the simple possession of a steak knife on one occasion, regardless of its use, can result in suspension or expulsion.

Arbitrary standards tend to be established by a minority of people (e.g., a school board) who have been given the authority to make decisions for the majority. Sometimes a single individual establishes the standards, as in the case of the classroom teacher: "You can only sharpen your pencil one time per class period."

Arbitrary standards are generally accompanied by good intentions. The school board wants to minimize violence in schools; the teacher wants to minimize aimless wanderings in the classroom. Furthermore, arbitrary standards might lead to positive results (e.g., a decrease in weapons—broadly defined—brought to school, an increase in time on task in the classroom). Thus, arbitrary standards are not necessary bad; they are just arbitrary.

Considered Standards

Considered standards are established when groups of people get together to talk, discuss, and deliberate about the standards that should be set. In setting standards on various high-stakes assessments, for example, people may be brought together to examine the individual tasks included on the assessment.

They may be asked to determine how many of the response options on each task included on a multiple-choice test could be eliminated by students who know very little about the content or objectives being assessed (Nedelsky, 1954). The result is the odds of getting each item correct by guessing. For example, if a student can eliminate two response options on a four-option multiple-choice item as being obviously wrong, his odds of getting the item correct by guessing are one of two or 50%. These resultant percentages are summed across all items to establish a minimal performance standard.

Alternatively, they may be asked to determine what proportion of a minimally competent group of students would likely respond correctly to each task (Angoff, 1971). The performance standard in this case is the sum of these percentages.

Another approach, one not requiring an item-by-item examination, is to ask teachers to identify students who they believe have and have not mastered the objectives being assessed. Two score distributions are prepared: one for those designated as *masters* and the other for those designated as *nonmasters*. The point of intersection between these two score distributions is chosen as the performance standard (Berk, 1976).

Regardless of the procedure used, careful attention is given to each assessment task as it pertains to one or more groups of students or to the perceived level of achievement of the students. Considered standards are an advance over arbitrary standards because people have come together to talk about them. Rather than resulting from a top–down or lone wolf process, they emerge as the result of a bottom–up process. That is, they are grounded in the concerns and opinions of those most likely to be affected by the standards.

Success-Oriented Standards

As their name suggests, success-oriented standards are those set in such a way as to increase students' chances of success in the future. Most approaches to standard setting have a here-and-now orientation. That is, based on what I know about my students and the assessment instrument, what level of performance will I accept as indicating that my students have learned what I expected them to learn? This is a reasonable question to ask within a present-oriented context. There is another question that can be asked, however—one with a future orientation. What level of performance do my students need to attain on this assessment instrument to have the best chance of being successful on later learning and assessment tasks and in later years? This is a more difficult question to ask partly because it requires longitudinal information (i.e., information collected on the same students over time). However, we can see the value of success-oriented standard setting by considering an example.

Virtually everyone has come to accept that early language development is a key to long-term educational success. Good, Simmons, and Kame'enui (2001) conducted a series of studies examining changes in oral reading fluency (ORF) during the early grades (1–3) as well as the relationship between third-grade ORF and performance on the Oregon Statewide Assessment (OSA). The data they collected provide an illustration of both the promise of setting success-oriented standards as well as the procedure involved in setting them.

Good, Simmons, and Kame'enui assessed the ORF of over 300 students at the end of the third grade and then compared their ORF scores with their scores on the OSA. To assesses ORF, the Test of Oral Reading Fluency (TORF; Children's Educational Services, 1987) was individually administered. Students were asked to read each of three passages aloud for 1 minute. Omitted words, substituted words, and hesitations of more than 3 seconds were scored as errors. If a student self-corrected within 3 seconds, the initial error was not counted. The median number of correct words per minute from the three passages was used as the ORF rate. A graphic summary of the results is shown in Fig. 6.2. The OSA scores are shown on the vertical dimension, and the TORF scores are shown on the horizontal dimension.

Several pieces of information are needed to understand the graph. First, the State of Oregon has established preset standards on the OSA. Students must attain a score of 201 for them to *meet expectations*. Furthermore, students who attain a score of 215 are said to *exceed expectations*. These two performance standards as shown as bold horizontal lines in Fig. 6.2. The problem, then, is to set a standard on the TORF in such a way that students who achieve the standard are very likely to be successful on the OSA (i.e., they either meet or exceed expectations).

Two possible performance standards are indicated in Fig. 6.2 by bold vertical lines. The lower of these two standards equates with a TORF score of 70. Students who achieve this score can read aloud at a rate of 70 words a minute without errors (or somewhat more than 70 words a minute when errors are made). The higher of these two standards equates with a TORF score of 110. This corresponds with an oral reading rate of 110 words per minute without error (or, again, a slightly higher rate if errors are made).

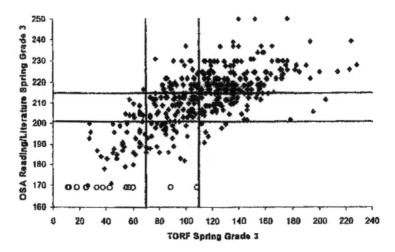

FIG. 6.2   Scatterplot relating oral reading fluency at Grades 3 with student performance on the Oregon Statewide Assessement (grade 3). Lawrence Erlbaum Associates. Reprinted with permission.

Of the 198 students with TORF scores of 110 or higher, 191 (96%) met expectations on the OSA. In contrast, of the 46 students with TORF scores below 70, 13 (28%) met expectations on the OSA. Thus, a TORF score of 110 is certainly a success-oriented standard. That is, students scoring above 110 are very likely to be successful on the OSA. Potential standards between 70 and 110 should certainly be examined. For example, from the graph it appears that the standard could be lowered to 100 with little decrease in the success rate on the OSA. To continue with this example, however, we assume a success-oriented standard of 110. Also, because of space limitations, we move down to first and second grades.

Figure 6.3 shows a plot relating TORF scores for the same students when they were in the first (horizontal dimension) and second (vertical dimension) grades. Once again, two possible standards for second-grade TORF scores are shown in the figure. The lower standard corresponds with a TORF score of 50, and the higher standard corresponds with an TORF score of 90. Keep in mind that our standard for third grade is a TORF score of 110. The question becomes how to set a standard in first grade that enhances the likelihood of success in second-grade, which, in turn, enhances the likelihood of success in third-grade, ultimately resulting success on the third-grade OSA.

A reasonable place to start is a first-grade TORF score of 40 (as indicated by the bold vertical line in Fig. 6.3). Of the 98 students who attained a TORF score of 40 in first grade, 95 (97%) attained a TORF score of 90 or higher in second grade. All 98 of these students attained a TORF score of 50 or higher

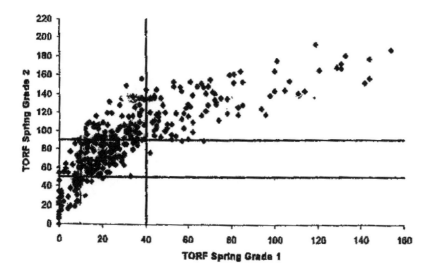

FIG. 6.3   Scatterplot relating oral reading fluency at Grades 1 and 2.   Lawrence Erlbaum Associates. Reprinted with permission.

in second grade. Thus, a first-grade TORF score of 40 is a success-oriented standard. Once again, the possibility of setting a slightly lower standard may be considered. For example, a first-grade standard of 35 may be a possibility.

In light of this example, we see that the setting of success-oriented standards begins with a clear, long-term, often externally imposed standard. In the example, this ultimate standard was meeting expectations on the OSA. First-, second-, and third-grade oral reading fluency standards were set to increase the success rates of students on the OSA. These standards were set initially at oral reading fluency rates of 40 in first grade, 90 in second grade, and 110 by the end of third grade. Modifications in these standards could certainly be made as illustrated earlier and also when additional information becomes available.

USING MULTIPLE COMPARISONS

Different comparisons are likely to be needed to make different decisions. For example, comparisons with other students may be needed to determine which students to place into a relatively costly instructional program such as Reading Recovery. After all, the resources provided by this program should be used with students who have the greatest need. Note that the phrase *greatest need* virtually calls for a norm-referenced interpretation to be made.

Even when there is a close alignment between type of comparison and type of decision, however, other comparisons may be useful to either corroborate or enhance the initial interpretation. Staying with the Reading Recovery example for the moment, a comparison with an underlying continuum would likely provide useful information on where to start the instruction with each student. Similarly, a comparison with a preset standard would likely provide useful information concerning when the student should leave the program and return to the regular class.

The point to be emphasized here is that these different approaches to interpretation should be viewed as complementary, not competitive. We should have moved beyond the time when criterion-referenced tests were the good guys and norm-referenced tests were the bad ones. Sound decision making is difficult enough without throwing away tools to aid in the decision-making process because they are not in vogue or politically correct.

CHAPTER SEVEN

Grading and Other Decisions

The purpose of this chapter is to explore some of the key decisions teachers make on the basis of assessment results. The title of the chapter reflects, in part, the long-standing relationship between assessment and grading. Traditionally, the primary purpose of student assessment has been to assign grades to students. In addition to grading, however, teachers use assessment information to make referrals, curricular decisions, and instructional decisions. Assigning grades and making referrals are decisions that require information about individual students. In contrast, curricular and instructional decisions require information about groups of students, quite often about entire classrooms or schools. Before discussing these decisions, however, let us begin by considering three principles of sound decision making based on assessment results.

BASIC PRINCIPLES: THE THREE Cs

In chapter 1, I made the statement that information was a necessary but not sufficient condition for good decision making. That is, simply having good information does not guarantee that a good decision will be made, but it helps. There are three principles that, when followed, result in a tighter connection between information and decision making and, ultimately, should result in more informed and defensible decisions being made. Because all of these principles begin with the letter C, they are collectively known as the three Cs. They are consistency, corroboration, and consideration of consequences.

Consistency

Better decisions tend to be made when consideration is given to the consistency of the information on which the decision is based. In chapter 1, *consistency* was mentioned as a synonym for *reliability*. Reliable information is information that remains stable across settings, tasks, and time. Decisions made on the basis of reliable information are likely to be better decisions.

Yet there is another aspect of consistency that is related to sound decision making. This consistency is based on change, not stability. An example
would be an economist who says, "There has been a consistent increase in
the price of consumer goods over the past six months." A consistent increase? Is this some type of oxymoron? Not at all. Mathematics would probably refer to it as a linear increase. Suppose, for example, the price of
consumer goods increased one half of 1% every month for the last 6
months. If you graphed this increase over the 6-month period, you would
get a straight line—hence, linear. Linear increases permit fairly reliable
(consistent) predictions to be made.

How is brief lesson in economics relevant to teachers? Suppose you
have to make a decision about an individual student based on his or her
classroom behavior. The issue before you is whether the student's behavior has improved over time. You decide to collect information via formal
observation. Specifically, you decide to focus your attention on the number of times the student interrupts the lesson, either by physical movement or verbal comments, over a 2-week period. Before making your
decision, you decide to graph your assessment results. Now consider the
two graphs shown in Fig. 7.1. Which graph would lead you to have more
confidence in your decision: the top or bottom one? If you have followed
the discussion thus far, the answer is the bottom one. More important,
the mean number of disruptions per day over the 2-week period is identical for the two graphs—4.8. If you did express more confidence in the
bottom graph, you did so based on the consistency of improvement, not
the overall amount of improvement. Considering consistency of information, whether defined in terms of stability over setting, tasks, and time or
in terms of predictable patterns of change over time, is likely to result in
better decisions being made.

Corroboration

Better decisions tend to be made when consideration is given to corroborating the information on which the decision is to be based. There is an important difference between verification and corroboration. To *verify*
means to establish the truthfulness of the information. To *corroborate*
means to strengthen or support the information. Although truth may, at
times, be an elusive concept, corroboration is something we all should do.

Corroboration means that we check to see whether others see things
the way we do. Corroboration means that we compare our information
with other available information. Finally, corroboration means that we
recognize that our information and the way we see things are fallible. Perceptions are not reality; perceptions are filtered through the lens that we
use to view reality.

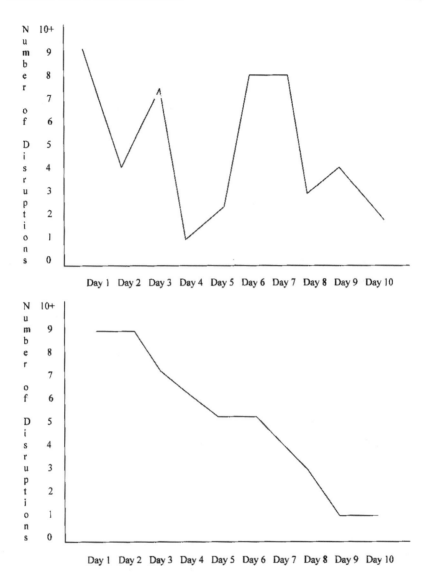

FIG. 7.1   Two patterns of classroom behavior.

Corroboration can come from many sources. We can consult permanent records. We can talk with parents. We can engage in discussions with our teaching colleagues. We can listen to students. Whatever the source, however, corroboration tends to produce better decisions.

Consideration of Consequences

Better decisions tend to be made when the person making the decision considers the consequences of the decision in advance of actually making it. What will happen if …? This question is the starting point for considering the consequences of our decisions. What will happen if I recommend suspension of this student? What will happen if I talk to the parents about this student's behavior? What will happen if I give students 10 points for putting forth effort (although they have not learned what I expected them to learn)? What will happen if I slow down the pace of instruction to accommodate those students who are having difficulty keeping up?

As novices our considered consequences are speculative. As a novice I have no way of knowing what is likely to happen if I give 10 extra points for effort. After a few years of experience, however, my anticipated consequences are increasingly supported by actual ones. It is at this point in the teacher's career that considered consequences are likely to result in better decisions being made.

In the previous paragraph, I used the phrase *likely to result in better decisions*. I recently observed a classroom in which a child would simply not comply with any of the teacher's requests or directives. Finally, in exasperation, the teacher told the child to "go and stand in the hall" and escorted the child to the classroom door. As she walked past me, she said in a low voice, "That's the fifth time he's had to stand in the hall this month." So what are the consequences of deciding to send the child to the hall? First, he loses valuable instructional time (although, quite clearly, he was not making use of it before). Second, and more relevant to the point made here, there apparently has been no improvement in his classroom behavior as a result of this practice in the past. Good decision considering the consequences? I think not.

GRADING STUDENTS

Although some teachers find grading students to be complex, ambiguous, and distressing, teachers are responsible for assigning grades to their students. In this section, four questions are addressed: Why grade? What should grades represent? What are the criteria for a sound, defensible approach to grading? What guidelines can be offered for developing a sound, defensible approach to grading?

Why Grade?

There are three primary reasons for grading students. First, grades are the primary currency of exchange for many of the opportunities and rewards our society has to offer. Grades can be exchanged for such diverse entities as adult approval, public recognition (when the local newspaper publishes the school's Honor Roll), college and university admissions (particularly when students apply for more selective colleges and universities), and even cash (when parents pay their children some amount of money for each "A" on their report cards). To deprive students of grades, therefore, is to possibly deprive them of rewards (in the present) and opportunities (in the future).

The second reason for grading students is habit. Students are used to receiving grades, and teachers are used to giving them. In fact, some students even equate grades with learning. To deprive teachers of grading and students of grades, therefore, is to ask them to break a deeply ingrained habit. For some students, it is to face the frightening possibility that they will have no way of knowing whether they have in fact learned.

The third reason for grading students is to motivate and control students. Grades can serve as incentives: "If you answer 85% of the questions correctly, you will get an 'A.'" For many students, incentives serve a motivating function. Grades can also be used as sanctions. "Those who received a grade lower than a 'B' on their homework will stay in during recess to correct their mistakes."

What Should Grades Represent?

Several times previously, the point has been made that teachers are concerned with three things: classroom behavior, effort, and achievement. In chapter 2, I mentioned that elementary school report cards tend to require that separate grades be given to each of these. Early on in school (Grades 1–3), the grades may be Commendable, Satisfactory, and Needs Improvement, or Achieving, Developing, and Not Yet. By Grade 4, however, traditional letter grades are usually in place. By middle school, concerns for classroom behavior, effort, and achievement have typically merged into a single grade for each subject area. Thus, middle and high school teachers have a bit of wiggle room in assigning grades. Good effort can increase a grade by one letter or at least add a "+" to the letter. Inappropriate classroom behavior can have the opposite effect, lowering a grade by half a grade or more.

Beginning about Grade 6, grades **can** represent many things, but the question being asked is normative: What **should** a grade represent? The answer to this question is inherent in the definition of grading. *Grading* is the process by which descriptive assessment information is translated into marks or letters that indicate the quality of a student's classroom behavior, effort, or achievement (Airasian, 1997). A grade should represent the quality of a student's classroom behavior *or* his or her effort *or* his or her achievement. That is, separate grades should be given for each of these. Furthermore, a grade should be based on the descriptive assessment information available to the teacher at the time that grades are assigned. That is, there must be a clear connection between the assessment information and the grade assigned. Having a clear connection between assessment information and grades allows the teacher to make the critical distinction between teachers giving grades and students earning grades. Students must earn achievement grades by virtue of their performance on the various assessment tasks. If this is not the case—if teachers began to manipulate this assessment–grading connection—they have put themselves in the position of giving grades rather than students earning them. This is a difficult position indeed.

What Are the Criteria for a Sound, Defensible Approach to Grading?

Different people have suggested different criteria for designing a sound, defensible grading system (Airasian, 1997; Gallagher, 1998; Gredler, 1999; McMillan, 1997). However, three criteria are common to all: meaningfulness, explicitness, and fairness.

Meaningfulness.   Meaningfulness means that everyone concerned understands what the grades signify. "A good grade means that I learned something." "A good grade means I worked hard." "A good grade means that I didn't cause trouble." Combining classroom behavior, effort, and achievement into a single grade decreases the meaningfulness of the grade. Having separate grades for classroom behavior, effort, and achievement increases the meaningfulness of the grades. Thus, based on the criterion of meaningfulness, separate grades are preferable to a composite grade.

Even when a grade is based exclusively on achievement data, a profile of data (as shown in Table 3.6, chap. 3) may be more meaningful than a total score. As the data included in Table 3.6 indicate, a total score can often be misleading even when there is a high degree of internal consistency reliability present.

Explicitness.   Explicitness means that everyone concerned understands how the teacher arrived at the grade. What information was considered? How was the information combined? How was the continuum of information translated into grading categories? The criterion of explicitness, then, pertains to both grading criteria and procedures.

Fairness.   The key to fairness is that each student has an equal opportunity to earn a grade. Notice that fairness does not mean that each student will receive a good grade or a high grade. Rather, it is possible that any given student can receive a good grade (or a bad grade for that matter). Using the criterion of fairness, norm-referenced grading (also known as grading on the curve) is blatantly unfair. A certain percentage of students is preordained to receive high grades, low grades, and average grades.

What Guidelines Can Be Offered for the Design of a Sound, Defensible Approach to Grading?

McMillan (1997) developed a set of guidelines—presented as a parallel set of dos and don'ts—that are useful in this regard. These guidelines are consistent with the three criteria mentioned before: meaningfulness, explicitness, and fairness. That is, when these guidelines are followed, the chances of designing a sound, defensible grading system are increased substantially. These guidelines are summarized in Table 7.1. The meaning of the first three guidelines (those indicated by asterisks) should be self-evident in light of the previous discussion. Consequently, I restrict my remarks to the last three guidelines.

TABLE 7.1
Dos and Don'ts of Effective Grading

Do	Don't
*Do everything you can to grade fairly	Allow personal bias to affect grades
*Grade students based on their achievement of important objectives	Grade on the curve using the class as the norm group; lower grades for misbehavior, lack of effort, tardiness, or absence
*Inform students and parents of grading procedures at beginning of year or semester	Keep grading procedures secret
Rely on most current information	Penalize students who perform poorly early in the year or semester
Use a sufficient number of assessments	Rely on one or two assessments for a quarter or semester grade
Make informed professional judgments	Depend entirely on number crunching; be inflexible with borderline cases

Note. From McMillan (1997).

Rely on Most Current Information.   Suppose Herman does extremely poorly on the first unit assessment. Furthermore, suppose that three unit assessments determine the quarter grade. Is Herman doomed to a grade of "C" because of his poor start or is it possible for Herman to earn a grade of "B" or, perhaps, "A"? If all unit assessments constitute one third of the total grade, Herman, in fact, may be doomed. Furthermore, if Herman realizes he is doomed this early in the quarter, what reason is there for Herman to expend effort for the remainder of the quarter? In this situation, early grades are likely to have a negative impact on student motivation.

What alternatives does a teacher have? There are two. The first is to grade on improvement over time. As Airasian (1997) pointed out quite clearly, however, there are several problems with this approach. First, students who do well on the first unit assessment have little room to improve. Second, there is an incentive for students to *play dumb* so that their early performance is low and improvement can be more easily shown.

The second alternative is to allow students to eliminate the lowest assessment performance and base the grade on the others. This alternative is preferable because it neither penalizes late starters nor gives students an opportunity to play dumb. In fact, those who play dumb early have greater pressure to perform at higher levels on later assessments. One other point, however: Just to play it safe, it may be wise to tell students that their performance on the final unit assessment counts no matter what. You do not want students tanking the final assessment because they have already earned an "A."

Use a Sufficient Number of Assessments.   In general, it is bad practice to base important decisions on a single piece of information. Clearly, there are exceptions to this rule. It only takes one cold-blooded killing to decide that a person is a murderer. Fortunately, however, these exceptions are rare indeed. Within any marking period, teachers should have at least three major assessments. In addition to the major assessments, teachers may choose to include homework assignments or in-progress work in the grading process. If so, these should carry much lower weights in the overall scheme of things (probably no more than 10%). Having multiple assessments increases the reliability of the information on which the grading decision is based.

Make Informed Professional Judgments.   To paraphrase a quotation made famous by the National Rifle Association (NRA), information does not make decisions, people make decisions. The argument put forth in this book is that these decisions should be guided in some way by useful information and made in a professionally defensible manner. The shorthand way of summing this up is in the phrase *informed professional judgments*.

In making informed professional judgments, teachers should avoid two common mistakes. The first is to put too much faith in the numbers. I have met teachers who are convinced they can tell the difference between an essay receiving a score of 93 and one receiving a score of 94. Although I admire these teachers for their confidence in themselves and their abilities, I have to admit that I find them to be delusional. In my 35 years in education, I have often had difficulty differentiating an "A" paper from a "B" paper, let alone a 93 from a 94. We often ascribe more precision to numbers than they deserve just because they are numbers. This pseudoprecision of numbers enables some teachers to abdicate their responsibility for decision making. "Your tests were computer scored and you had 28 correct. If you look at the grading scale I gave you before the test, 28 is a C+." End of story!

The second mistake that teachers make in this regard is to forget what grades are supposed to mean. Because we are human, we often find it difficult to give high grades to lazy students regardless of how well they performed. It does not seem right somehow. Alternatively, we do not mind giving a few extra points to students who work hard (but do not learn) or at least who behave well in class. Cheating ... well, cheating can only be punished by assigning lower grades. Obviously, cheating is a very serious offense, but what does it have to do with grading?

Cheating means that the use of the information gained from the assessment is null and void. That is, it does not count. As McMillan (1997) pointed out, because cheating is a serious offense, "an appropriate disciplinary action is warranted. However, lowering grades is not an appropriate discipline because of the extreme negative impact it may have on the grade.... It would be better to find another kind of punishment and [re-assess] the student" (p. 318).

REFERRING STUDENTS

There are times in every teacher's life when he or she comes to a realization: "I just don't know what to do to help this student." At this point in time, the teacher starts to look for people who can help and situations in which the student can be more successful. The teacher recognizes the need to refer the student to other people or situations. In terms of classroom behavior, the referral is often to a specific person (e.g., principal, guidance counselor). In terms of achievement, the referral is more likely to be to a specific program (e.g., special education, local academic tutoring program). Regardless of the person or program to whom the student is referred, the decision to refer is a crucial and difficult decision for most teachers.

In some cases, teachers must follow a well-defined referral process. To refer a student for special education placement, for example, a sequence of steps must be followed. The referral process for special education placement in the state of Missouri is shown in Table 7.2. The process begins with screening (i.e., specific problem identification). However, before a student can be referred for more formal evaluation (Step 3), attempts must be made to accommodate the student in the regular classroom by means of alternative instructional and/or behavioral management strategies. In the special education literature, these are referred to as *prereferral intervention strategies* (Step 2).

In other cases, teachers have a great deal of discretion in making referrals. The decision to send a student to the principal's office or to see the guidance counselor is solely the teacher's decision. Regardless of the nature of the problem or the person or program to which the student is being referred, several guidelines should be followed by the classroom teacher. These guidelines are summarized briefly next.

Never Refer a Student in Frustration or Anger

I began this discussion of referral decisions with a hypothetical quote from a teacher. "I just don't know what to do **to help** this student." I could have written the quote as follows: "I just don't know what to do **with** this student." In reality, I have heard the second quote far more often than the first. The second quote is more realistic because inherent in it is the frustration that many teachers feel at the time they say it. Despite this frustration, teachers must keep in mind that referrals are intended to help students, not hurt them. That is, referrals are intended to place students with people and in situations where they can get the help they apparently are not receiving in the regular classroom.

TABLE 7.2
Referral Process for Special Education Placement in Missouri

1.	Screening
2.	Referral Intervention Strategies
3.	Referral and Screening Interview
4.	Individual Evaluation Plan Development
5.	Notice and Consent for Evaluation
6.	Evaluation
7.	Diagnostic Summary
8.	Individual Education Plan Development
9.	Notice and Consent for Placement

Note. From University of Missouri-Columbia (1990).

A similar point can be made about referrals to the principal's office. I would suggest that many of these referrals are made in anger. When referrals are made in anger, the long-term negative consequences far outweigh the immediate positive effect of "not having to deal with that student any more today." The student is embarrassed in front of his or her peers; the teacher is embarrassed in front of his or her students (after all, Ms. Smith lost her temper). It is unlikely that the relationship between teacher and student(s) will ever be the same.

When calmness prevails, it may be apparent that a meeting with a counselor is more likely to be productive than a meeting with the principal. If so, the teacher can meet with the counselor and suggest that he or she schedule an appointment with the student. Regardless of the decision made, decisions made in frustration or anger are rarely the best decisions.

Consider the Consequences of the Referral Decision

Quite obviously, this is a special case of the third "C"—namely, consider the consequences. Suppose a teacher decides to send a student to the principal's office. That may in fact solve the teacher's immediate problem. With that student removed from the classroom, the teacher and remaining students can get back to the task at hand. Yet what about tomorrow and the next day? What is the long-term impact of that referral decision?

Suppose that a teacher decides to recommend a student for placement in a special education program. Furthermore, suppose that somewhere along the multistep referral process, a decision is made that the student will not be placed in a special education program. Perhaps the results of the formal evaluation do not support placement. Perhaps the parents do not give consent for placement. How has the teacher's relationship with the student changed as a result of the teacher's decision to recommend the student for placement in the first place?

By suggesting the need to consider the consequences of referral decisions, I am not suggesting that all consequences are negative, nor that considering the consequences should move teachers away from making the necessary decision. Rather, I am suggesting that better decisions are made when some consideration is given to the consequences before, rather than after, the decisions are made. Once a decision is made, it is difficult to go back.

Base Referrals on Recurrent Patterns of Behavior

The signs and indicators of a student's need for counseling or special education placement are many and varied. They do have one thing in common, however. They tend to recur over time. Many students have skirmishes with their classmates. Only those for whom these skirmishes have become a regular part of their school day should be considered for referral. Many students have difficulty with a particular unit in history, science, literature, or mathematics. Only those who have difficulty on almost every unit should be considered for referral. Thus, in accordance with the first C principle, consistency of inappropriate behavior, lack of effort, and/or poor achievement should be a key consideration in making a referral decision.

Be Able to Link Decisions With Specific Assessment Information

A sound, defensible decision requires that there is a clear connection between the decision and the specific information on which the decision was based. A form such as the one shown in Fig. 7.2 can be used to make this

Name of Student:	Date:
Name of Teacher:	
Briefly Describe Referral Decision:	

Reason(s) for Decision (check all that apply)	
	Poor grades
	Decreasing grades
	School work of poor quality
	Low test scores
	Frequent tardiness
	Frequent absenteeism
	Disruptive behavior
	Immature, suggestible behaviors
	Difficulty getting along with peers
	Fails to pay attention in class; easily distracted
	Fails to turn in classwork or homework
	Other (describe)

For each reason checked above, give specific examples (including dates and times, if appropriate. For grades, test scores, tardiness, and absenteeism, attach copies of records. For poor quality school work, attach examples. Write on back of form as needed.

FIG. 7.2 Sample form for documenting reasons for referral decisions.

connection explicit. The reasons listed are actually categories of reasons (e.g., school work of poor quality). The reverse side of the form plus attachments are intended to provide specific examples within each category. For *school work of poor quality*, for example, various daily assignments completed by the student can be attached.

MAKING CURRICULAR AND INSTRUCTIONAL DECISIONS

Teachers make numerous curricular and instructional decisions on a daily, weekly, monthly, and yearly basis. Several examples of these decisions were mentioned in chapters 1 and 2. In an attempt to make sense of the variety of decisions that teachers made and to suggest how assessment results can be used to inform these decisions, Nitko (1989) identified four types of teacher decisions: placement, diagnostic, monitoring, and attainment.

Placement Decisions

Placement decisions are made at the beginning of a semester- or year-long course. The purpose of these decisions is to place students, according to their prior knowledge or other learning prerequisites, into a sequence of instructional units at an appropriate level. Thus, placement decisions require teachers to understand two things about their students. First, how much of what the students have been exposed to in the curriculum in previous years have they retained? Second, how much of what I intend to teach them in this course do they already know? The answers to these questions require that some form of assessment be conducted.

Some have argued that the information contained in students' permanent records, combined with a knowledge of the scope and sequence of the curriculum, provides the information needed to answer these questions. I suggest that this is not the case for two reasons. First, information contained in students' permanent records is somewhat dated (McMillan, 1997). The issue is not what the students knew last April. Rather, it is what students know in mid-August or early September. Second, the scope and sequence of a curriculum indicates what **should be** taught to students. There is ample evidence that the *curriculum on paper* and the *curriculum in practice* are two quite different things (Westbury, 1989).

Spending the first week of a semester- or year-long course assessing students would seem a wise investment of time. The results of these assessments can provide valuable information about what students know and are able to do prior to beginning instruction. In this way, objectives already mastered can be eliminated from the curriculum, resulting in more time for those objectives on which students traditionally have difficulty.

Affective assessments can also be included during this time frame. The results of these assessments can provide useful information about those characteristics that are aligned with positive, prosocial classroom behavior, and motivation and effort. Finally, with older students, these should be formal assessments. As mentioned in chapter 5, a great deal of potentially useful information can be obtained by administering an affective assessment battery. With younger students, they are more likely to be informal, perhaps taking the form of assessment conversations (Anderson et al., 2001).

Diagnostic Decisions

Diagnostic decisions are based on information indicating which objectives have and have not been attained by the students. Furthermore, they are based on what are believed to be the reasons for success or failure and, as a consequence, represent the basis for what has been termed *corrective instruction* (Block, Efthim, & Burns, 1989). Initially, then, diagnostic decisions rely primarily on information obtained from the assessment of student achievement. If diagnostic decisions are to be made based on this information, however, the interpretation should be made in terms of the underlying achievement continuum or an objective-by-objective examination in terms of preset standards. Little diagnostic information is available from interpretations based on comparisons with other students.

Determining the reasons for success or failure requires that the instruments used to assess student achievement provide as much information as possible about what students both know and do not know. When selection tasks are used, for example, care must be taken in the choice of the response options to include. The incorrect response options chosen by reasonably large numbers of students can provide useful clues as to the why of the failure.

Generally speaking, extended response tasks provide more useful information on which to base diagnostic decisions. This point is nicely illustrated in two examples provided by Perrone (1991):

> [The item on the New York City test] asked, "Which of the following trees can be found growing along the streets of our city? a) Redwood, b) Palm, c) Rubber, d) Maple." While not suggesting that the question was unimportant, the teachers asked in their alternative test, "Name some trees that grow along the streets of New York" The 30 3rd-grade children who took the alternative test named 73 different species of trees (including the "Central Park tree"). For instructional purposes, teachers gained entry points they hadn't thought about. Rather than ask, as the city-wide test did, "Which of the following planets is the largest? a) Venus, b) Mars, c) Pluto, d) Jupiter," the test prepared by the teachers asked students to draw a picture of the solar system. The drawings were enormously revealing. (p. 7)

Finally, the reasons for failure to achieve on a given assessment may lie outside the realm of academic learning. Rather, the reasons may be related to a lack of effort or an inability to pay or sustain attention in class. The information needed to explore these possible reasons is likely to come from observations and affective assessment instruments.

Monitoring Decisions

Monitoring decisions are based on data concerning whether instructional activities are meeting instructional goals, posing unexpected difficulties, or should be altered. As mentioned several times previously, monitoring decisions are based primarily on teachers' observations of student engagement and time on task. However, daily or weekly seatwork assignments provide useful information as well. The earlier that instructional and learning problems are identified, the earlier attempts can be made to solve them. In so many respects, then, early identification and intervention are the keys to effective instruction and successful learning.

Attainment Decisions

Attainment decisions relate to a final evaluation of the achievement of important unit or course objectives. Such decisions are almost always based on formal assessment of student achievement. Once again, interpretations based on comparisons with an underlying continuum, comparisons based on preset standards, or both should be used to make these decisions. Comparisons with other students generally provide little information about the attainment of unit or course objectives.

CONCLUDING COMMENT

Informed professional judgment is one of the most important qualities a teacher can possess and exhibit. Regardless of the decision being made, getting the necessary information and using it deliberately are critically important. In this regard, consistency, corroboration, and considering consequences are three Cs that increase the likelihood of using information to make sound, defensible decisions.

CHAPTER EIGHT

Communicating Assessment Results

In this closing chapter, we explore some of the ways in which assessment results can be communicated effectively to parents and other interested parties. The word *explore* in the previous sentence was chosen carefully because the discussion of this topic in this chapter is more of a survey of possibilities than an in-depth treatment. The purpose of this chapter is to remind the reader of the importance of communication in explaining the decisions made on the basis of assessment results.

The most traditional means by which assessment results are communicated to parents is by means of report cards. Even parents, however, tell us that report cards leave much to be desired. In a pair of studies, parents reported that parent–teacher conferences provided much more useful information about their child and their child's progress than did report cards (Shepard & Bleim, 1995; Waltman & Frisbie, 1994). Both report cards and conferences provide information about individual students. How can teachers communicate assessment results about groups of students? Fortunately, technological advances have enabled teachers to use newsletters and Web sites to communicate group-based information. Before discussing report cards, conferences, newsletters, and Web sites, however, let us begin by considering three principles of effective communication.

BASIC PRINCIPLES: THE THREE Fs

Just as decision making is improved by applying the three Cs, the quality of communication is increased by following the three Fs: focus, friendliness, and forthrightness.

Focus

Most people find rambling communication tiresome and onerous. People who talk aimlessly and seemingly endlessly are aggravating. Reading print material where you keep asking yourself, "What's the point?" is annoying. Focus in communication means simply that (a) you have a point, and (b)

160

you stay on point. Focus in communication requires planning and preparation. It also means being sufficiently disciplined to control any tendencies to wander aimlessly or engage in what is called *bird walking* by educational and communication consultants.

Friendliness

Friendliness is used here in the sense that the phrase *user-friendly* is used in the computer world. In the larger context of communication, we are talking about being audience friendly. To be audience friendly, you first have to know your audience. Permanent files provide a rich, often untapped source of information in this regard. As one elementary teacher stated:

> I always look at the parent's occupation to see if their parents are working outside the home ... which give me an idea of perhaps how hectic their schedules might be ... I look to see how much education the parents have ... so that I might weigh the experiences the child will get outside of school. (Davis, 1995, p. 157)

Knowing the audience also means being aware of the language spoken in the home. If the language of instruction is different from that spoken in the home, the child may be placed in the role of translator between the school and the parents. Because of the increasing number of non-English-speaking parents, many schools are hiring main office personnel who are multilingual.

Regardless of the language spoken in the home, *audience friendly* means using words that members of the intended audience can fully understand. Educationese is replete with jargon, acronyms, and abbreviation. "We need to obtain an initial EEN before we convene the M-team. If all is in order, the M-team will prepare a draft IEP." "Your son's NPR indicates that his reading performance is about average. But he tends to have difficulty in the areas of phomenic awareness and textual comprehension." If jargon, acronyms, and abbreviations must be used, the teacher should take time to educate the parents in their meaning.

Forthrightness

Synonyms for forthrightness are *honesty, frankness*, and *candor*. Forthrightness is important in communication because it enhances the credibility of what is written or said. Indirectly, then, forthrightness is important because a teacher's credibility in the community is determined in some part by their communication with members of the community. Forthrightness is enhanced when specific information about students is presented (e.g., work samples, exact days on which he or she was tardy, specific test scores clearly explained). Forthrightness is undermined when teachers try to bluff their way through. They do not know the answer, but they make one up. The preferred approach is to simply say, "I don't know, but I'll see if I can find out. I'll get back to you one way or another in three or four days."

REPORT CARDS

Despite the title of this section, this is not a discussion of report cards per se. Most teachers have little input into the structure and format of their report cards. Thus, discussing the ideal report card (even if there were one) would be a waste of time. After all, there is some truth to the saying, "If you've seen one report card, you've seen them all." This is particularly true the higher up the education system you go. Rather, this is a discussion of the limitations inherent in report cards and the value of written comments on report cards.

The Limitations of Report Cards

There are at least two major limitations of report cards. First, regardless of how grades are assigned, students and parents tend to use them normatively. Early on, both students and parents want to know how they (the students) stack up against their same-age or same-grade peers. I personally have heard concerns for high school rank voiced by parents of fourth-grade students.

Second, many students and parents (and some teachers) believe that grades are far more precise than they are. In most grading schemes, an "F" is any percentage below 75. This is an extremely large range of scores for one single grading category. To combat this problem, some teachers prefer to add pluses and minuses. Others prefer to use numerical grades (e.g., 76, 88).

These changes result in what can best be termed *pseudoprecision*. Keep in mind that there are errors in the assessment tasks. There are errors in the responses that students give to the tasks. There are errors in scoring the responses that students give to the tasks. There are errors involved in combining the results of multiple assessments within a grading period. There are errors involved in rounding. Despite the imperfect nature of assessment results, however, some people place great faith in the 87 or B+ they see on a report card. That is just the way it is and the way it will remain for some time to come.

The Value of Written Comments on Report Cards

Not only are grades imprecise, they are vague in their meaning. They do not provide parents or students with a thorough understanding of what has been learned or accomplished (Hall, 1990; Wiggins, 1994). Teacher comments, if done well, can convey the information not completely described by letter or number grades.

Well-written comments can offer parents and students suggestions as to how to make improvements in specific academic or behavioral areas. Furthermore, written comments provide teachers opportunities to be reflective about the academic and behavioral progress of their students. Such reflections may result in teachers gaining a deeper understanding of each student's strengths and needs for improvement.

Table 8.1 contains three lists of words and phrases, the first two of which can be incorporated into report card comments. The third list contains four words and phrases that should be avoided. *Always* or *never* should not be used because it only takes one exception to call the veracity of the comment into question. *Almost always* or *rarely* are much preferred.

TABLE 8.1
Words and Phrases to Include on and Exclude from Written
Comments on Report Cards

Words and Phrases that Promote Positive View of the Student

1. Gets along well with people
2. Has a good grasp of ...
3. Has improved tremendously
4. Is a real joy to have in class
5. Is well respected by his classmates
6. Works very hard

Words and Phrases to Convey That Student Needs Help

1. Could benefit from ...
2. Finds it difficult at times to ...
3. Has trouble with ...
4. Requires help with ...
5. Needs reinforcement in ...

Words and Phrases to Avoid or Use with Extreme Caution

1. Always
2. Never
3. Can't (or "is unable to ...")
4. Won't

Note. From Bruadli (1998).

Can't should not be used because teachers truly do not know what a student can or cannot do. Teachers only know what a student does (or doesn't do). "Can't" requires a causal explanation that few teachers should be willing to make without much more information being made available to them. Like *can't, won't* requires a causal explanation. In fact, going back to the task that Binet was given by the French Ministry of Education (see chap. 2), *can't* equates with a lack of ability and *won't* equates with a lack of motivation. In almost all situations, using *doesn't* is a safer bet when making written comments.

CONFERENCES

Parent–teacher conferences provide opportunities for flexible two-way communication, unlike the one-way communication that report cards provide. Conferences permit discussion and elaboration of students' classroom behavior, effort, and achievement. In addition, teachers can use conferences to gather information from parents about their (the parents') perceptions of and concerns about their sons or daughters. This information may be useful in explaining students' behavior, effort, and/or achievement. Finally, from a purely interpersonal perspective, conferences allow participants to attach faces to names. This initial attachment increases the likelihood of more positive communication in the future.

As suggested earlier, parents report that conferences are more useful and informative than any other form of communication (Shepard & Bleim, 1995). In fact, Waltman and Frisbee (1994) found that almost two of every five parents rated conferences as the single most useful source of information about their sons or daughters.

Table 8.2 contains a list of guidelines for conferences with parents. It should be pointed out, however, that the vast majority of these guidelines are appropriate for conferences in general. The entries in the table are divided into four sections: planning for conferences, what to discuss, conducting conferences, and mistakes to avoid.

Planning for Conferences

Planning is a process by which an individual visualizes the future and creates a framework to guide his or her actions in that future. One of the first steps in planning, then, is determining what you want to achieve. Next, you need to set forth a process for getting you there. Preparing an agenda is a necessary step in this regard. Finally, several of the agenda items likely require materials and data to discuss properly. Be sure all needed materials and data are ready and available.

TABLE 8.2
Guidelines for Conferences With Parents

Planning for Conferences

1. Know what you want to achieve

2. Prepare an agenda

3. Have all the materials and data that you need

What to Discuss

1. Both status and progress in areas of achievement, effort, and classroom behavior

2. Be as specific as possible without being overly detailed

Conducting Conferences

1. Conduct conference in private, quiet, comfortable setting

2. Greet parents, welcome them, and say something positive about their son or daughter

3. Establish an informal, yet professional tone

4. Foster parent participation; encourage them to ask questions; engage in conversation and avoid lecturing

5. Be frank and honest

6. Near the end of the conference, identify two or three areas in which improvement is needed; determine responsibilities for each area

7. After the conference has ended, write a note to the parents thanking them for attending the conference and summarizing the next steps

Mistakes to Avoid

1. Avoid using educational jargon, acronyms, and abbreviations

2. Avoid bluffing; say you do not know

3. Avoid making promises you cannot keep

4. Avoid discussing other students or teachers

What to Discuss

The question of what to discuss is derived in large part from the overall purpose of the conference. Is the purpose to update parents on how well their son or daughter is doing in class? Was the conference called by the teacher in response to a continued behavioral problem? In the first situation, the focus should be on achievement, effort, and classroom behavior.

In the second, the focus, at least initially, should be on the specific behavioral problem that led to the conference in the first place.

In general, parents want to know not only how their child is doing, but whether there has been any change over time. Thus, both status and progress (or the lack thereof or regression) should be discussed. Similarly, parents tend to be uneasy with generalities. They want to know specific information supporting or illustrating these generalities. At the same time, however, you do not want to overwhelm parents with details. The general rule of thumb should be "some details, but not every detail." Select those details that make or reinforce the point or points you are trying to make.

Conducting Conferences

The seven entries in this section of Table 8.2 can be thought of as a sequence of steps. First, arrange a private, quiet, comfortable setting. Second, greet parents, welcome them, and say something positive about their son or daughter. Third, ..., and so on.

Most of these points should be reasonably clear in light of the previous discussion. A few are worthy of comment, however. Point 3, for example, suggests that teachers should establish an informal, yet professional tone. In terms of the three Fs mentioned earlier, this calls for merging friendliness with forthrightness. This is not an easy task. It is far easier to error on either side than to find a comfortable middle position.

Point 4 emphasizes the importance of active parent participation in the conferences. One sign of active participation is asking questions. There are at least two ways in which teachers can encourage parents to ask questions: (a) modeling questioning, and (b) reinforcing questioning. Modeling questioning means that you use questions frequently during the conference. This has a positive side effect—namely, it moves the conference from a lecture to a conversation.

Reinforcing questioning means that you attend to parents' questions immediately when asked and provide answers to the questions they can understand. The response, "That's an interesting question. Let's come back to it if we have time," is not reinforcing of questioning. What it does reinforce is that my agenda is more important than your questions. Teachers can also reinforce questioning by saying things such as, "You know, I was wondering that myself."

Point 6 is very important. A conference should be seen as an opportunity for continuing conversation, not as a one-time thing. In addition, parent conferences allow teachers to enlist parental support—to build a team to help students achieve their goals (Airasian, 1997). A focus on two or three areas keeps things manageable and avoids developing a laundry list (which would be impossible to complete) by getting priorities established. Finally, assigning responsibilities is an important step in linking talk with action.

Simple notes to parents (Point 7) keep the lines of communication open. In addition, writing and sending notes is a matter of professional courtesy. In today's high-tech world, it is not difficult to write and send these notes. Several templates for notes can be stored in a computer file as can mailing labels. Finally, having a written copy of agreed-on next steps provides the basis for subsequent parent conferences.

Mistakes to Avoid

Points 1 and 2 in this section of the table have been addressed earlier, the first in the context of our second F, fairness, and the second in the context of our third F, forthrightness. The other two points are worthy of additional comment. Many teachers find it tempting to either placate or comfort parents by telling them they are going to *do* something, *check* something, or *fix* something. Do not promise these things unless you are certain that you have the authority, resources (including time), and commitment to actually do, check, or fix.

Parents often initiate the last potential mistake on the list. "What about Trey's friend, Alex? He's doing no better than Trey, but he's getting Cs (not Ds)." "Ms. Torville (another teacher) told Trey that some of your requirements were just too difficult for many of the students." Do not get suckered into debates based on "he said, she said." It is simply good practice to not discuss any other students or teachers with parents, although it may be difficult to avoid in some instances.

Practical Problems

Despite the potential benefits associated with parent conferences, they are not without their practical problems. The three most frequently cited are scheduling, language barriers, and parents' previous school experiences (Gallagher, 1998). Increases in the number of working mothers and single-parent homes have made scheduling parent conferences far more difficult than it used to be. Similarly, increases in non-native English speakers (as mentioned earlier) have made it more likely that language will be a barrier in parent conferences. A drawback to at least some parents is that conferences usually take place on school grounds. Not all parents had positive experiences when they were in school and being back in that environment may conjure up some bad memories.

Whether these problems can be solved depends to a large extent on how important it is to solve them. Some teachers have met parents at convenient shopping malls on Saturdays or even at the students' homes in the evenings. Others have used the telephone when face-to-face conferences were not feasible. Similarly, language barriers may be somewhat overcome with the use of an interpreter, but the situation is still a bit awkward, and interpreters may not be readily available.

NEWSLETTERS AND WEB SITES

Both reports cards and conferences provide information about individual students. How can information about groups of students be communicated? Fortunately, the technology available today makes it relatively easy to provide up-to-date group-based information. What information should be provided? How should newsletters and Web sites be prepared to best provide this information? These are the two questions that are addressed in this final section of this chapter.

What Information?

A variety of information about assessment tasks, assessment instruments, and assessment results can be provided in newsletters and on Web sites. For example, sample assessment tasks can be provided on a regular basis to indicate concretely the learning expectations teachers have for their students. Similarly, the dates of major formal assessments can be given so that students and their parents are aware of them. In addition, information can be provided to help parents (and others) interpret the results of formal assessments (e.g., a column on percentile ranks, a question-and-answer column in which parents can submit questions). In today's word of educational accountability, an assessment newsletter seems worthy of consideration.

How to Prepare

Table 8.3 contains a set of guidelines for preparing newsletters and Web sites. Once again, several of these guidelines are reasonably clear in their intent and meaning. Thus, comments are reserved for a selected few.

Organize Material So That Things Are Easy to Find. Many newsletters represent a *pot pourri* of news and notes. People are asked to submit items, and the items are placed in the newsletter in the sequence in which are submitted. Because there is no overall structure to the newsletter, it reads more like a open letter to the community than a useful source of information. One solution to this problem is to use the same organizational structure from issue to issue. Introductory remarks from the teacher can be the opening story. Sample assessment tasks (complete with answers as well as how to arrive at the answers) can be placed on the top half of the back

TABLE 8.3
Guidelines for Newsletters and Web Pages

1. Determine purpose and intended audience.

2. Include only material and links that make sense for intended audience.

3. Focus on a few stories/themes.

4. Organize material so things are easy to find.

5. Connect pictures with text; avoid "pictures for the sake of pictures."

6. Avoid clutter.

7. Choose font to ensure readability, not cuteness.

8. Proofread all work carefully.

9. Keep Web sites current.

10. Indicate who should be contacted if questions arise.

page. The newsletter can end with the upcoming calendar of important dates. By using the same organizational structure from issue to issue, the newsletter becomes increasingly reader friendly.

In terms of Web sites, determine what information is of most use to most users. A formal or informal needs assessment can help in this regard. Many people use school Web sites to contact teachers and administrators. Thus, the directory link should be easy to locate on the home page.

Connect Pictures With Text; Avoid "Pictures for the Sake of Pictures."
Pictures are often used as decorations, rather than to enhance the information value of the material presented. Pictures should contribute to the understanding of the information presented, not detract from it. Cuteness may be cute, but it is not necessary informative.

Proofread All Work Carefully. There are some parents and community members who take it on themselves to correct every error they see in print. Some even seem to take great satisfaction in pointing them out. Do not give them the satisfaction. Proofreading is a tedious job, but one that conveys a sense of care and professionalism to many people.

Keep Web Sites Current. Any new technology is fun initially. In some cases, having a Web site is the modern day equivalent of "keeping up with the Jones." The question arises, "What happens when the newness wears off?" During my numerous excursions on the Internet, I frequently encounter Web sites that have not been updated for 3 or more years. If Web sites are worth setting up in the first place, they are worth maintaining.

CLOSING COMMENT

Once a decision has been made, it must be implemented. Implementing decisions generally requires some form of communication. Focused, friendly, and forthright communication has the potential not only of moving from thought and talk to action, but also the potential to marshal the resources needed to ensure that the action taken leads to the desired result.

References

Airasian, P. W. (1997). *Classroom assessment* (3rd ed.). New York: McGraw-Hill.

Anderson, L. W. (1991). *Increasing teacher effectiveness*. Paris: International Institute for Educational Planning.

Anderson, L. W., & Bourke, S. F. (2000). *Assessing affective characteristics* (2nd ed.). Mahwah, NJ: Lawrence Erlbaum Associates.

Anderson, L. W., Krathwohl, D. R., Airasian, P. W., Cruikshank, K., Mayer, R. E., Pintrich, P., Raths, J., & Wittrock, M. C. (2001). *A taxonomy for learning, teaching, and assessing: A revision of Bloom's taxonomy of educational objectives*. New York: Longman.

Anderson, v. Banks, 520 F. Supp. 472, 499-501 (S. D. Ga. 1981).

Angoff, W. H. (1971). Scales, norms, and equivalent scores. In R. L. Thorndike (Ed.), *Educational measurement* (2nd ed., pp. 508–600). Washington, DC: American Council on Education.

Arlin, M. (1979). Teacher transitions can disrupt time flow in classrooms. *American Educational Research Journal, 16*, 42–56.

Bartley, R. (1997). *The effect of access to test item pools on student achievement and student study habits*. Unpublished Ed. D. dissertation, Virginia Polytechnic Institute and State University.

Baron, J. B. (1991). Strategies for the development of effective performance assessment exercises. *Applied Measurement in Education, 4*(4), 305–318.

Barton, P. E. (1994). *Becoming literate about literacy*. Princeton, NJ: Policy Information Center, Educational Testing Service.

Berk, R. A. (1976). Determination of optimal cutting scores in criterion-referenced measurement. *Journal of Experimental Education, 45*, 4–9.

Block, J. H., Efthim, H. E., & Burns, R. B. (1989). *Building effective mastery learning schools*. White Plains, NY: Longman.

Bloom, B. S. (1981). *All our children learning*. NY : McGraw–Hill.

Boekaerts, M., Pintrich, P., & Zeidner, K. (Eds.). (2001). *Handbook of self-regulation*. New York: Academic Press.

Boreson, L. (1994). *A programming guide for emotional disturbance*. Madison, WI: Wisconsin State Department of Public Instruction. (ERIC Document Number 374 581)

Bradby, D. (1992). *Language characteristics and academic achievement: A look at Asian and Hispanic eight graders in NELS:88*. Washington, DC: U.S. Government Printing Office. (ERIC Document Number 343 971)

Brookhart v. Illinois State Board of Education, 534, F. Supp. 725, 728 (C.D. Ill. 1982).

Brophy, J. E., & Good, T. L. (1986). Teacher behavior and student achievement. In M. C. Wittrock (Ed.), *Handbook of research on teaching* (3rd ed., pp. 328–375). New York: Macmillan.

Brualdi, A. (1998). Teacher comments on report cards. *Practical Assessment, Research, & Evaluation, 6*(5). Accessible at ericae.net/pare.

171

Bussis, A. M., Chittenden, E. A., & Amarel, M. (1976). *Beyond surface curriculum.* Boulder, CO: Westview.

Calfee, R. C., & Masuda, W. V. (1997). Classroom assessment as inquiry. In G. D. Phye (Ed.), *Handbook of classroom assessment* (pp. 69–97). San Diego, CA: Academic Press.

Carroll, J. B. (1985). A model of school learning. In C. W. Fisher & D. C. Berliner (Eds.), *Perspectives on instructional time* (pp. 18–33). New York: Longman.

Children's Educational Services. (1987). *Test of reading fluency.* Minneapolis, MN: Author.

Clark, C. M., & Peterson, P. L. (1986). Teachers' thought processes. In M. C. Wittrock (Ed.), *Handbook of research on teaching* (3rd ed., pp. 255–296). New York: Macmillan.

Clay, M. M. (1993). *Reading Recovery: A guidebook for teachers in training.* Auckland, NZ: Heinemann Education.

Crandall, V. J., Katkovsky, W., & Crandall, V. C. (1965). Children's belief in their own control of reinforcement in intellectual-academic situations. *Journal of Consulting Psychology, 29,* 27–36.

Dahloff, U. S. (1971). *Ability grouping, content validity, and curriculum process analysis.* New York: Teachers College Press.

Davis, M. M. D. (1995). *The nature of data sources that inform decision making in reading by experienced second grade teachers.* Unpublished doctoral dissertation, Old Dominion University.

Doyle, W. (1979a). Making managerial decisions in classrooms. In D. Duke (Ed.), *Classroom management* (pp. 41–74). Chicago: University of Chicago Press.

Doyle, W. (1979b). Classroom tasks and student abilities. In P. Peterson & H. Walberg (Eds.), *Research on teaching* (pp. 184–213). Berkeley, CA: McCutchan.

Doyle, W. (1986). Academic work. In T. M. Tomlinson & H. J. Walberg (Eds.), *Academic work and educational excellence* (pp. 175–196). Berkeley, CA: McCutchan.

Emmer, E. T., & Evertson, C. M. (1981). Synthesis of research on classroom management. *Educational Leadership, 38*(4), 342–347.

Evertson, C. M., & Green, J. (1986). Observation as inquiry and method. In M. C. Wittrock (Ed.), *Handbook of research on teaching* (3rd ed., pp. 162–213). New York: Macmillan.

Feather, N. (Ed.). (1982). *Expectations and actions.* Hillsdale, NJ: Lawrence Erlbaum Associates.

Finn, J. D. (1989). Withdrawing from school. *Review of Educational Research, 59,* 117–142.

Fitzsimmons, G. W., Macnab, D., & Casserly, C. (1985). *Technical manual for the Life Roles Inventory Values Scale and the Salience Inventory.* Edmonton, Alberta: PsiCan Consulting Limited.

Fogarty, J. L., Wang, M. C., & Creek, R. (1982). *A descriptive study of experienced and novice teachers' interactive instructional decision processes.* Paper presented at the AERA annual meeting, New York City.

Fraser, B. J., Anderson, G. J., & Walberg, H. J. (1982). *Assessment of learning environments: Manual for Learning Environment Inventory (LEI) and My Class Inventory (MCI).* Perth, Australia: Curtin Institute of Technology.

Gallagher, J. D. (1998). *Classroom assessment for teachers.* Upper Saddle River, NJ: Merrill.

Gardner, R. C., & MacIntyre, P. D. (1993). On the measurement of affective variables in second language learning. *Language Learning, 43,* 157–194.

Glaser, R., & Nitko, A. J. (1971). Measurement in learning and instruction. In R. L. Thorndike (Ed.), *Educational measurement* (2nd ed., pp. 625–670). Washington, DC: American Council on Education.

Good, R. H., Simmons, D. C., & Kame'enui, E. J. (2001). The importance and decision-making utility of a continuum of fluency-based indicators of foundational reading skills for third-grade high-stakes outcomes. *Scientific Studies of Reading, 5,* 257–288.

Goodenow, C., & Grady, K. (1993). The relationship of school belonging and friend's values to academic motivation among urban adolescent students. *Journal of Experimental Education, 62,* 60–71.

Gredler, M. E. (1999). *Classroom assessment and learning.* New York: Longman.

Gronlund, N. (2002). *Assessment of student achievement* (2nd ed.). Boston : Allyn & Bacon.

Hall, K. (1990). *Determining the success of narrative report cards.* Unpublished manuscript. (ERIC Document Number 334 013)

Herman, J. L. (1997). Large-scale assessment in support of school reform: Lessons in the search for alternative measures. *International Journal of Educational Research, 27,* 395–413.

Jackson, P. W. (1968). *Life in classrooms.* New York: Teachers College Press.

Jessor, R., & Jessor, S. (1977). *Problem behavior and psychosocial development.* New York: Academic Press.

Joint Committee: American Federation of Teachers, National Council on Measurement in Education, and National Educational Association. (1990). The standards for teacher competence in the educational assessment of students. *Educational Measurement: Issues and Practices, 9*(4), 29–32.

Kehoe, J. (1995). *Writing multiple-choice test items.* Washington, DC : ERIC.

Kirisci, L., & Moss, H. B. (1997). Reliability and validity of the Situational Confidence Questionnaires in an adolescent sample. Confirmatory factor analysis and item response theory. *Measurement and Evaluation in Counseling and Development, 30,* 146–155.

Kounin, J. S. (1970). *Discipline and group management in classrooms.* New York: Holt, Rinehart & Winston.

McMillan, J. H. (1997). *Classroom assessment.* Boston: Allyn & Bacon.

Medley, D. M. (1982). Teacher effectiveness. In H. E. Mitzel (Ed.), *Encyclopedia of educational research* (5th ed., pp. 1330–1334). New York: The Free Press.

Moos, R. H., & Trickett, E. J. (1987). *Class Environment Scale manual* (2nd ed.). Palo Alto, CA: Consulting Psychologists Press.

Nedelsky, L. (1954). Absolute grading standards for objective tests. *Educational and Psychological Measurement, 14,* 3–19.

Nitko, A. J. (1989). Designing tests that are integrated with instruction. In R. Linn (Ed.), *Educational measurement* (3rd. ed., pp. 447–474). New York: Macmillan.

North Dakota Department of Public Instruction. (1999). *Guidelines: Evaluation process.* Bismarck, ND: Author. (ERIC Document Number ED 443 204)

Nowicki, S., Jr., & Strickland, B. R. (1973). A locus of control scale for children. *Journal of Consulting and Clinical Psychology, 40,* 148–154.

O'Neill, R. E., Horner, R. H., Albin, R. W., Sprague, J. R., Storey, K., & Newton, J. S. (1997). *Functional assessment and program development for problem behavior: A practical handbook* (2nd ed.). Pacific Grove, CA: Brooks/Cole.

Osterman, K. F. (2000). Students' need for belonging in the school community. *Review of Educational Research, 70,* 323–367.

Perrone, V. (1991). *ACEI position paper on standardized testing*. Washington, DC: Association for Childhood Education International.

Phillips, S. E. (1994). High-states testing accommodations : Validity versus disabled rights. *Applied Measurement in Education, 7,* 93–120.

Pintrich, P. R., Smith, D. A. F., Garcia, T., & McKeachie, W. J. (1991). *A manual for the use of the Motivated Strategies for Learning Questionnaire (MSLQ)*. Ann Arbor, MI: The Regents of the University of Michigan.

Plucker, J. A. (1996). Construct validity evidence for the Student Aspirations Survey. *Journal of Research in Rural Education, 12,* 161–170.

Popham, W. J. (1994). *Anonymity enhancement procedures for classroom affective assessment*. Paper presented at the annual meeting of the American Educational Research Association, New Orleans.

Pressey, S. L., & Pressey, L. C. (1922). *Introduction to the use of standard tests*. Yonkers-on-Hudson, NY: World Book Company.

Rabinowitz, W., & Travers, R. M. W. (1953). Problems of defining and assessing teacher effectiveness. *Educational Theory, 3,* 212–219.

Roderick, M. (1993). *The path to dropping out*. Boulder, CO: Westview.

Ryans, D. G. (1960). Prediction of teacher effectiveness. In C. W. Harris (Ed.), *Encyclopedia of educational research* (3rd ed., pp. 1486–1491). New York: Macmillan.

Schiefele, U., & Csikszentmihalyi, M. (1995). Motivation and ability as factors in mathematics experience and achievement. *Journal for Research in Mathematics Education, 26,* 163–181.

Scriven, M. (2000). *The logic and methodology of checklists*. Address given at Claremont Graduate University, June. (Available at www.wmich.edu/evalctr/checklists)

Shavelson, R. J. (1973). *The basic teaching skill: Decision making*. Stanford, CA: Stanford University School of Education Center for R & D in Teaching.

Shepard, L., & Bliem, C. (1995). Parents' thinking about standardized tests and performance assessment. *Educational Researcher, 24*(8), 25–32.

Smith, J. K., Smith, L. F., & DeLisi, R. (2001). *Natural classroom assessment*. Thousand Oaks, CA: Corwin Press.

Squires, D. A., Huitt, W. G., & Segars, J. K. (1983). *Effective schools and classrooms: A research-based perspective*. Alexandria, VA: Association for Supervision and Curriculum Development.

Stiggins, R. J. (2001). *Student-centered classroom assessment* (3rd ed.). Columbus, OH: Macmillan.

Stipak, D. J. (1986). Children's motivation to learn. In T. M. Tomlinson & H. J. Walberg (Eds.), *Academic work and educational excellence* (pp. 197–222). Berkeley, CA: McCutchan.

Sugai, G., Lewis-Palmer, T., & Hagan. S. (1998). Using functional assessments to develop behavior support plans. *Preventing School Failure, 43*(1), 6–13.

Thorndike, E. L. (1910). Handwriting. *Teachers College Record, 2*(2).

Tobin, T. J. (1994). *Behavior challenges: A teacher's guide to functional assessment*. Eugene, OR: University of Oregon, College of Education, Behavior Disorders Program.

University of Missouri-Columbia. (1990). *Referral, identification, placement: The Missouri special education process, Revised*. Columbia, MO: Author. (ERIC Document Number 326 007)

Waltman, K. K., & Frisbee, D. A. (1994). Parents' understanding of their children's report card grades. *Applied Measurement in Education, 7*(3), 241–251.

Weiner, L. E. (1994). *Increasing frequency and appropriateness of high school teachers' referrals for speech language support services by implementing a public relations campaign.* Unpublished Ed. D. Practicum Report, Nova Southeastern University. (ERIC Document Number 372 547)

Westbury, I. (1989). The problems of comparing curriculums across educational systems. In A. C. Purves (Ed.), *International comparisons and educational reform* (pp. 17–34). Washington, DC: Association of Supervision and Curriculum Development.

Wiggins, G. (1994). Toward better report cards. *Educational Leadership, 52*(2), 28–37.

Wiggins, G. (2000). Glossary. (See www.relearning.org)

Glossary

Accommodations. Modifications in the way assessments are designed or administered so that students with disabilities and limited English proficient students can be included in the assessment. Examples include Braille forms for blind students or tests in native languages for students whose primary language is other than English.

Achievement. What a student knows and is able to do at a particular point in time as a result of school-based instruction.

Affective Assessment. Assessment of beliefs, emotions, and feelings, such as values, interests, attitudes, and self-esteem.

Alignment. The extent to which objectives, assessments, and instructional activities are connected with one another. For example, do the assessments match the objectives? Are the instructional activities likely to lead to mastery of the objectives?

Alternative Assessment. An assessment that requires students to generate a response to an assessment task, rather than choose from a set of responses provided to them. Alternative assessments consist of extended response tasks.

Anchor. A sample of student work that exemplifies a specific level of performance. Anchors are used to assign a numerical value to student performance on one or more assessment tasks. On a five-point scale, for example, there would be five anchors. Anchors are essential to objectivity when extended response tasks are used in assessment.

Assessment. The process of gathering and interpreting information to aid in classroom decision making.

Assessment Battery. A collection of assessment instruments, typically administered at or near the same time, that provides the range of information needed to make an informed decision.

Assessment Task. See *Task.*

Benchmark. A detailed description of a specified level of student performance expected of students at particular grades, ages, or development levels. Benchmarks are frequently used to monitor progress toward meeting long-term learning goals within and across grade levels.

Bias. Results that advantage one person or group over another based on factors other than the primary characteristic or quality being assessed (e.g., gender, race, native language).

Checklist. A set of criteria, each of which is said to be met or not met by the response(s) made by students to assessment tasks.

Criteria. Qualities, characteristics, or dimensions used to judge the quality of student responses to assessment tasks. Criteria indicate what we value in student responses to these tasks.

Difficulty. See *Task Difficulty.*

Discrimination. The extent to which students who answer a particular question (or other assessment task) correctly also receive higher scores on the total assessment instrument. Discrimination indexes are used to determine whether individual assessment tasks belong on assessment instruments.

Evaluation. Judging the quality of something, such as student learning, program success, or school effectiveness.

Extended Response Tasks. Tasks that require students to create a response, typically a response of some duration in terms of the number of words or time.

Formal Observations. Observations that are typically scheduled and made with the use of a structured observation form or schedule.

Formative Assessment. Assessment made for the purpose of gathering information that can be used by teachers to improve instruction or by students to improve learning.

High-Stakes Assessment. Assessments, the results of which are used to make major decisions about individuals, such as grade promotion, awarding of diplomas, and placement in special education.

Informal Observations. Spontaneous observations made without a structured observation form or schedule.

Introductory Material. Visual or verbal information that students need to respond to an assessment task.

Item. An individual assessment task.

Key. A list of the right answers (e.g., correct, best) to each assessment task included on an assessment instrument.

Learning. A change in student achievement over time.

Learning Task. See *Task.*

Logical Error. The use of irrelevant information to evaluate a student's classroom behavior, effort, or achievement.

Measurement. The process of assigning numbers to the assessment of various student characteristics or qualities (e.g., classroom behavior, effort, achievement).

Norm Group. The group of students to whom a particular student is being compared. Also the group of students who were tested to produce the norms for a commercial achievement test. Norm groups are also known as *Normative Samples* or *Reference Groups.*

Norm-Referenced Interpretations. Interpretation of a student's assessment results in terms of the assessment results of other students.

Normative Sample. See *Norm Group.*

Norms. Distributions of test scores of large samples of students, typically students at a particular grade level. On commercial achievement tests, these distributions take the shape of a normal or bell-shaped curve. Norms provide the basis for norm-referenced interpretations of test scores.

Objective. A statement that describes an intended and/or desired student accomplishment that occurs as a result of instruction. The statement includes a verb that indicates the intended cognitive process (e.g., understand, apply) and a noun or noun phrase that indicates the knowledge (e.g., conceptual, procedural).

Objectivity. The extent to which the results of an assessment are free from observers, scorer, or rater error.

Observations. See *Formal Observations; Informal Observations.*

Percentile Rank. A number that indicates the percentage of students scoring equal to or lower than a particular student or group. For example, if Billy has a percentile rank of 87 on some commercial achievement test, this indicates that 87% of the students with whom he is being compared scored the same as or lower than he did.

Performance Assessment. An assessment of a student's observable performance on some task. Tasks may include building a scale model of a village or swimming 500 meters using the butterfly stroke.

Portfolio. A well-defined collection of student work that shows changes in student achievement over time.

Rating Scale. See *Scale.*

Raw Score. The total number of points earned by a student on an assessment instrument; the total number of items a student answered correctly on a test.

Reference Group. See *Norm Group.*

Reliability. The degree to which the results of an assessment are dependable and consistent over time, tasks, and/or settings.

Response. The answer a student gives (or is expected to give) or the performance he or she exhibits (or is expected to exhibit) when given an assessment task (e.g., writing an answer, selecting an answer).

Response Options. The choices that a student is given in a selection task.

Rubric. A scoring guide that enables scorers or raters to make reliable judgments about the quality of student responses made to extended response tasks. Rubrics include explicit criteria, an underlying continuum for each criterion, and verbal descriptions connoting differences in the quality of student responses.

Scale. A continuum laid out in terms of quantitative or qualitative differences. There are five-point scales (quantitative) and there are scales that range from *poor* to *excellent* (qualitative). Student responses to assessment tasks are placed on the continuum, and the appropriate number or word is assigned to the response. The process assigning tasks to the continuum is referred to as rating; hence, *rating scales.*

Scoring Rubric. See *Rubric.*

Selection Tasks. Tasks that require students to choose the correct or best response from among the alternatives or options provided.

Standardized. A uniform set of procedures for administering and scoring an assessment. The purpose of standardization is to ensure that all students are assessed under the same conditions so that comparisons between and among their score have meaning.

Standards. The broadest of a family of terms referring to statements of learning expectations for students. There are content or curricular standards (also known as *objectives*), performance standards (which answer the question, "How much is enough?"), and benchmarks (see *Benchmarks*).

Stanine. A numerical value pertaining to the normal distribution or bell curve that groups students into nine categories.

Stem. The part of an assessment task that contains the question, incomplete statement, or directive.

Task. A goal and a set of activities designed to achieve the goal. If the goal is to facilitate student learning of explicit objectives (i.e., content or curricular standards), we call the task a *learning task*. If the goal is to determine what or how well students have learned explicit objectives, we call the task an *assessment task*. In either case, the activities are typically in the form of questions to be answered or directives to be followed.

Task Difficulty. The percentage of students who give the correct or best answer or otherwise successfully perform a task.

Test. A set of assessment tasks typically administered to a group of students in a specific time period.

Test Battery. See *Assessment Battery*.

Validity. The degree to which assessment information permits correct interpretations of the characteristic or quality being assessed (e.g., classroom behavior, effort, achievement); the extent to which assessment information is appropriate for making the desired decision.

Author Index

Subject Index

A

Accommodation, 18–20
Achievement, 26, 44
    assessment and, 27–37
    assessing using extended response and
        performance tasks, 72–95
    assessing using selection and short-an-
        swer tasks, 48–71
Affective assessment, 115–122
    designing affective assessment instru-
        ments, 120–122
    tasks, 131–132
    writing directions for, 122
    writing statements for, 121
Alternative assessments, 72–73
Anchors, 87–88, 125
Authentic assessment, 72–73
Assignments, 9
Assessment
    and decision making, 20–22, 156–157
    and ethics, 15–16
    and evaluation, 22
    as applied social science, 21–22
    definition of, 4
    formative, 45
    preparing students for, 16–18
    reasons for, 23–26
    summative, 46
    timing of, 43–47
Assessment instruments, 62–65
    administration of, 64–65
    analyzing results of, 65–70, 94
    determining appropriate length, 49–52,
        78, 80
    development over time, 71
    interpreting results of (see Interpretation
        of assessment results)
    preparation of, 62–64
    structure of, 68–69
Assessment tasks, 7–9
    anatomy of, 52–57

    contrasted with learning tasks, 9
    extended response and performance,
        72–95
    form vs. substance, 55, 57
    reviewing, 61–62
    selection and short-answer, 48–71
    scoring, 63–64, 70, 83–95
    writing, 52, 56–61, 80–83

B

Benchmarks (see Performance standards)
Causal models, 108–120
    and assessment, 111–113
    and functional behavioral assessment,
        113–115

C

Cheating, 153
Checklists, 83–87
    criteria of merit, 85
    definition, 83
    diagnostic, 85–87
    for student involvement, 102–103
    sequential, 84–85
    value of, 84
Classroom behavior, 26
    assessing, 42–43
    understanding problem classroom be-
        havior, 118–120
Communicating assessment results, 160–170
    conferences (see Conferences)
    guidelines, 166, 169
    focus of, 160
    forthrightness in, 160–162
    friendliness in, 160
    newsletters, 168–170
    report cards (see Report cards)